C000235944

CONTENTS

REFERENCE

MOTORWAY	M1
Under Construction	
Proposed	
MOTORWAY JUNCTIONS WITH NUMBERS	
Unlimited interchange 6 Limited interchange 7	
MOTORWAY SERVICE AREA	WOODALL
with access from one carriageway only	S
MAJOR ROAD SERVICE AREAS	LEEMING
with 24 hour Facilities	S
PRIMARY ROUTE _ (with junction number)	A55 32
PRIMARY ROUTE DESTINATION	RIPON
DUAL CARRIAGEWAYS (A & B Roads)	
CLASS A ROAD	A675
CLASS B ROAD	B5248
MAJOR ROADS UNDER CONSTRUCTION	
MAJOR ROADS PROPOSED	
SAFETY CAMERAS WITH SPEED LIMITS	
Single Camera	30
Multiple Cameras located along road	50
Single & Multiple Variable Speed Cameras	V V
GRADIENT 1:5(20%) & STEEPER (Ascent in direction of arrow)	«
TOLL	TOLL
MILEAGE BETWEEN MARKERS	8
RAILWAY AND STATION	
LEVEL CROSSING AND TUNNEL	
RIVER OR CANAL	
COUNTY OR UNITARY AUTHORITY BOUNDARY	
NATIONAL BOUNDARY	+
BUILT-UP AREA	
VILLAGE OR HAMLET	o
WOODED AREA	
SPOT HEIGHT IN FEET	• 813
HEIGHT ABOVE SEA LEVEL 400' - 1,000' — 122m - 305m	
1,000' - 1,400' — 305m - 427m	
1,400' - 2,000' — 427m - 610m	
2,000' + — 610m +	
NATIONAL GRID REFERENCE (Kilometres)	100
AREA COVERED BY TOWN PLAN	SEE PAGE 86

TOURIST INFORMATION

AIRPORT	
AIRFIELD	
HELIPORT	
BATTLE SITE AND DATE	✕ 1066
CASTLE (Open to Public)	
CASTLE WITH GARDEN (Open to Public)	
CATHEDRAL, ABBEY, CHURCH, FRIARY, PRIORY	
COUNTRY PARK	
FERRY (Vehicular)	
(Foot only)	
GARDEN (Open to Public)	
GOLF COURSE ____ 9 HOLE ____ 18 HOLE ____	
HISTORIC BUILDING (Open to Public)	
HISTORIC BUILDING WITH GARDEN (Open to Public)	
HORSE RACECOURSE	
INFORMATION CENTRE	i
LIGHTHOUSE	
MOTOR RACING CIRCUIT	
MUSEUM, ART GALLERY	
NATIONAL PARK OR FOREST PARK	
NATIONAL TRUST PROPERTY (Open)	NT
(Restricted Opening)	NT
NATURE RESERVE OR BIRD SANCTUARY	
NATURE TRAIL OR FOREST WALK	
PLACE OF INTEREST ____ Monument •	
PICNIC SITE	
RAILWAY, STEAM OR NARROW GAUGE	
THEME PARK	
VIEWPOINT ____ 360 degrees	
180 degrees	
VISITOR CENTRE	
WILDLIFE PARK	
WINDMILL	
ZOO OR SAFARI PARK	

SCALE

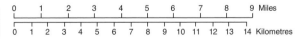

1:221,760
3.5 Miles to 1 Inch

Geographers' A-Z Map Company Ltd
Fairfield Road, Borough Green,
Sevenoaks, Kent TN15 8PP
01732 781000 (Enquiries & Trade Sales)
01732 783422 (Retail Sales)
www.a-zmaps.co.uk
Edition 2 2008
Copyright © Geographers' A-Z Map Company Ltd.

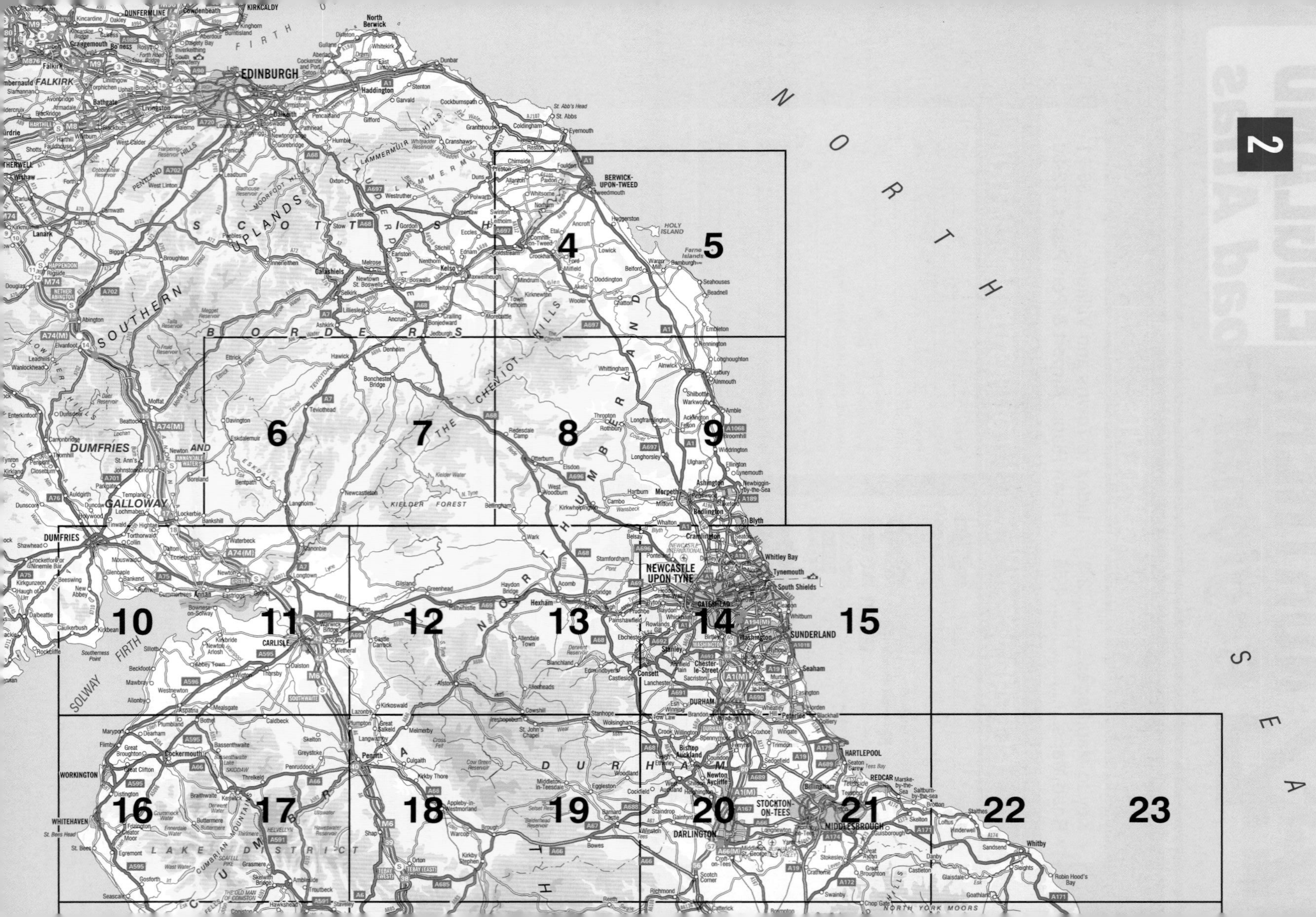

NORTHERN ENGLAND
Road Atlas

N O R T H   S E A

NORTH

23
22
21
20
19
18
17
16
15
14
13
12
11
10
9
8
7
6
5
4

NEWCASTLE UPON TYNE

BERWICK-UPON-TWEED

CARLISLE

DUMFRIES

SUNDERLAND

HARTLEPOOL

MIDDLESBROUGH

STOCKTON-ON-TEES

DARLINGTON

WORKINGTON

WHITEHAVEN

EDINBURGH

FALKIRK

CHEVIOT HILLS

KIELDER FOREST

NORTHUMBERLAND

THE BORDERS

LAMMERMUIR HILLS

SOUTHERN UPLANDS

SOLWAY FIRTH

LAKE DISTRICT

CUMBRIAN MOUNTAINS

DURHAM

NORTH YORK MOORS

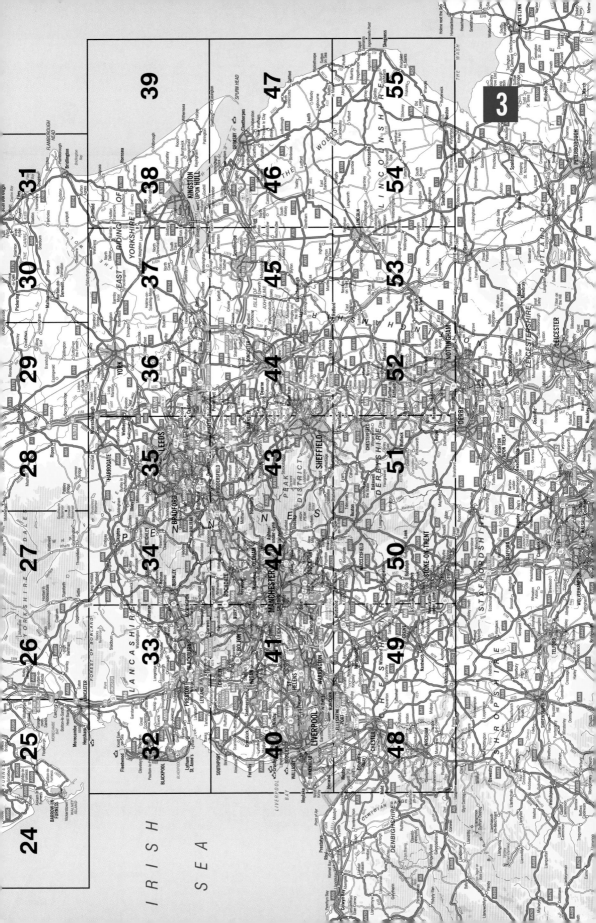

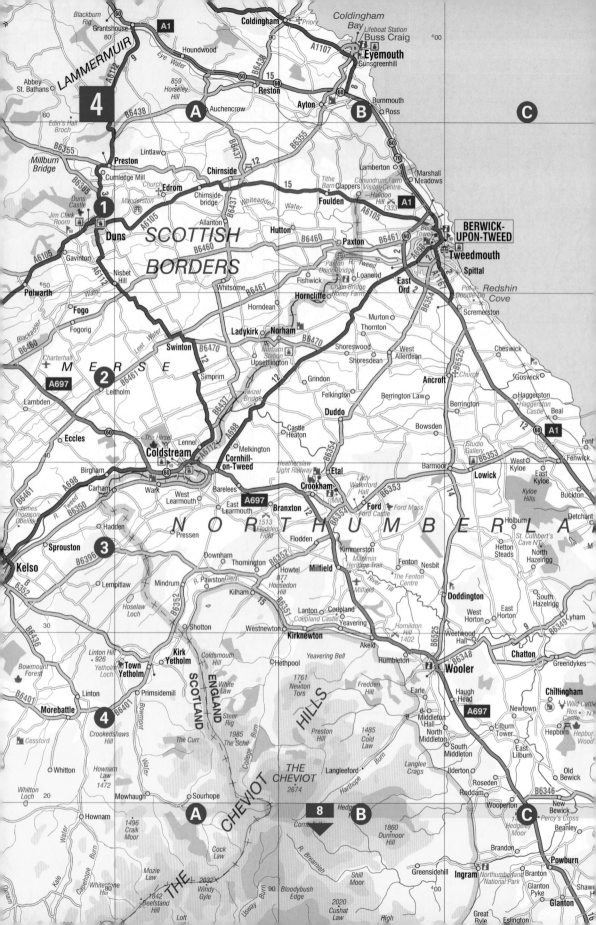

D   E   F   **5**

20   30   40   60

1

N   O   R   T   H

6 50

S   E   A   **2**

LINDISFARNE
HOLY ISLAND
Keel
Head   40

sfarne
e Centre   **Holy**
Island
arne   *Priory*   *NT Lindisfarne*
Castle Point

Burrows
Hole

Longstone

NT   **3**

Elwick   Ross   **Budle**   *Staple*
D   *Bay*   *Sound*   **FARNE**
Waren   B1342   Chapel NT   **ISLANDS**
Mill   **Bamburgh**   *Inner*   NT
Easington   Budle   B1340   *Sound*   *Farne*
  Grace   *Islands*
Spindlestone   *Darling*   Burton   New   NT
Bradford   Shoreston
ADDERSTONE   Elford   **North**   **Seahouses**
Bellshill   S   **Lucker**   *Seahouses NT*   *Heritage*
B6348   60   Adderstone   **Sunderland**   Carr End
30

A1   Warenford   Newham   Swinhoe   9   **Beadnell**
Lime
Kilns NT
West   West   *Beadnell*
Fleetham   Fleetham   *Bay*
Chathill   Tughall
Ellingham   Preston   *Snook Point*
High Newton-
by-the-Sea   **4**
Middle   Brunton   Low Newton-
Moor   *Preston*   by-the-Sea
Tower   *Newton Pool NT*
North   Doxford   Christon   *Embleton*
Charlton   Bank   **Embleton**   *Bay*
Armstrong   B6347   *Embleton*   **Dunstanburgh**
Household   *Tower*   NT
& Farming   South   20
Charlton   Rock   Dunstan   **Craster**
pe   60   *Memorial*
Eglingham   **D**   **E**   **9**   **F**
B6341   **Rennington**   Stamford
Heiferlaw   Littlemill   Howick
Tower   **A1**   9   *Howick*
East Bolton   Shipley   *Hall*
Hulne   Littlehoughton
Priory
R.   *Hulne*   Denwick   **Longhoughton**
Ain   *Park*   *Alnwick*
Bolton   *Abbey*   20   Boulmer
1093
ALNWICK   **A1068**   30   40

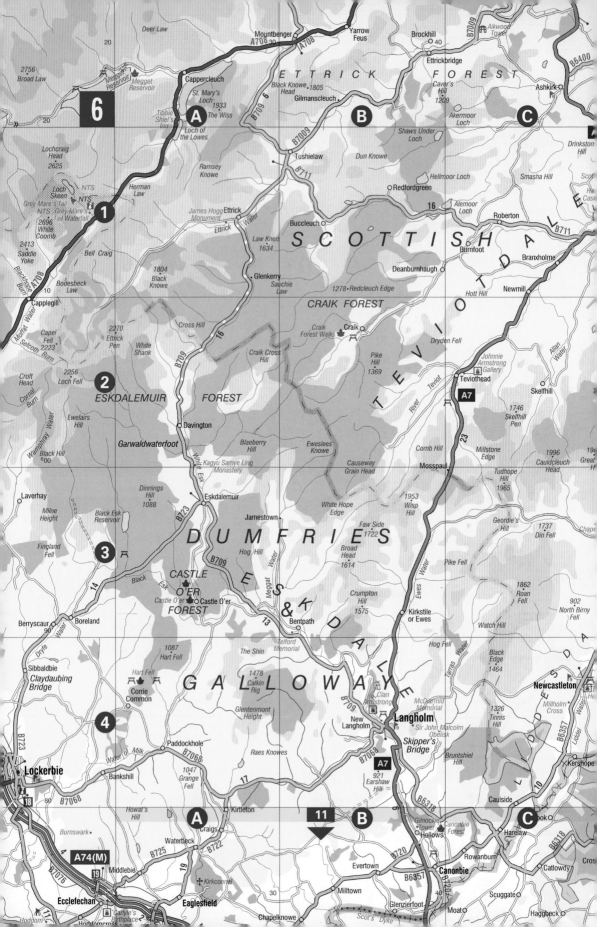

15

D   E   F

H

Newcastle to:
Amsterdam (IJmuiden) 15hrs.
Bergen 26hrs.
Haugesund 21hrs. 30mins.
Stavanger 18hrs. 30mins.

N O R T H

rsden Bay
den
Souter NT
Lizard Point
Whitburn
Colliery
Whitburn

South
Bents
Seaburn

Roker
onkwearmouth
National Glass Centre

SUNDERLAND SEE PAGE 78

Hendon

A1018

Ryhope
Colliery
Ryhope

Church
eside **SEAHAM**
Dawdon
**Dalton-
le-Dale**

Cold A182
Hesledon
EASINGTON
Hawthorn   Beacon Point

**Easington
Colliery**

Easington   Horden
Point

Horden
Dene Mouth

PETERLEE   Blackhall
Colliery
Castle   **Blackhall
Eden   Rocks**
High
Hesleden   Crimdon
Eden Vale   Monk   Park
Hesleden
tation   **Hart
Town   Station**

A19   *Church*
Hutton
Henry
Sheraton   **Hart**
B1280   West
A179   View
Middleton

S E A

1

2

3

4

D   E   21   F

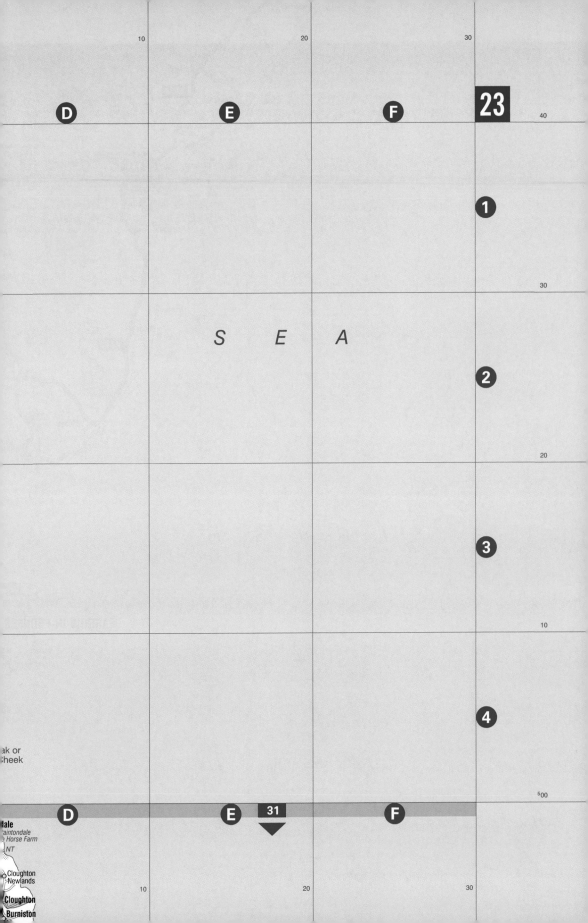

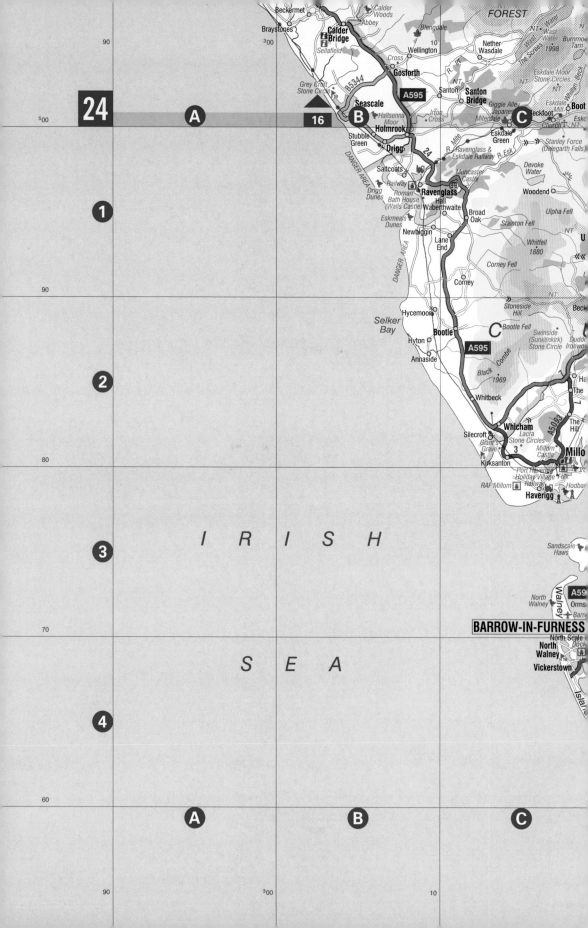

D   **E**   **F**   **31**

1

N O R T H

90

S E A

2

80

3

70

4

60

F

D   **E** 38 ▼   **F**

oak or
cheek

dale
Staintondale
Horse Farm
NT

Cloughton
Newlands
Cloughton
Burniston
71
A165
Scalby Mills
Sea Life & Marine Sanctuary
Newby
Barrowcliff
SCARBOROUGH
Falsgrave
Spa Cliff Lift
B1427
A170
A165
A64
Osgodby
NT
Crossgates
Eastfield
Cayton Bay
B1261
Cayton
The Wyke
B1261
Lebberston
Gristhorpe
Newbiggin
A1039
Filey
Folk
Filey
Flixton
Folkton
Muston
Primrose Valley
Staxton
A1039
Royal Oak
Hunmanby Sands
Hunmanby
Orchard Farm Railway
H I R E
Fordon
Reighton
Wold Newton
Speeton
Bempton Cliffs
B1229
FLAMBOROUGH HEAD
Foxholes
Burton Fleming
Buckton
Bempton
Danes Dyke
B1253
Bridlington
Grindale
Marton
Thwing
A165
Sewerby Hall
Flamborough
Octon
Sewerby
B1255
Bondville Miniature Village
Boynton
B1259
B1253
BRIDLINGTON
Langtoft
Rudston
Rudston Monolith
Gypsey Race
Harbour
West Hill
Hilderthorpe
EAST RIDING
Carnaby
Bessingby
West End
Kilham
Burton Agnes Hall
John Bull World of Rock
Wilsthorpe
Haisthorpe
Bridlington Bay
Burton Agnes
Norman Manor House
Thornholme
Carnaby
A614
Ruston Parva
Harpham
Fraisthorpe
OF YORKSHIRE
Lowthorpe
Gransmoor
D
Nafferton
Little Kelk
E Barr 38 ▼
A164
DRIFFIELD
Great Kelk
Lissett
B1242
East End
Gembling
Howe
West End
Ulrome
Wansford
Foston on the Wolds
Cruckley Animal Farm
Skipsea
Skerne
A165
Dringhoe
Skipsea
B1249
Beeford
Upton
Skipsea Brough
Hutton
Brigham
B1249

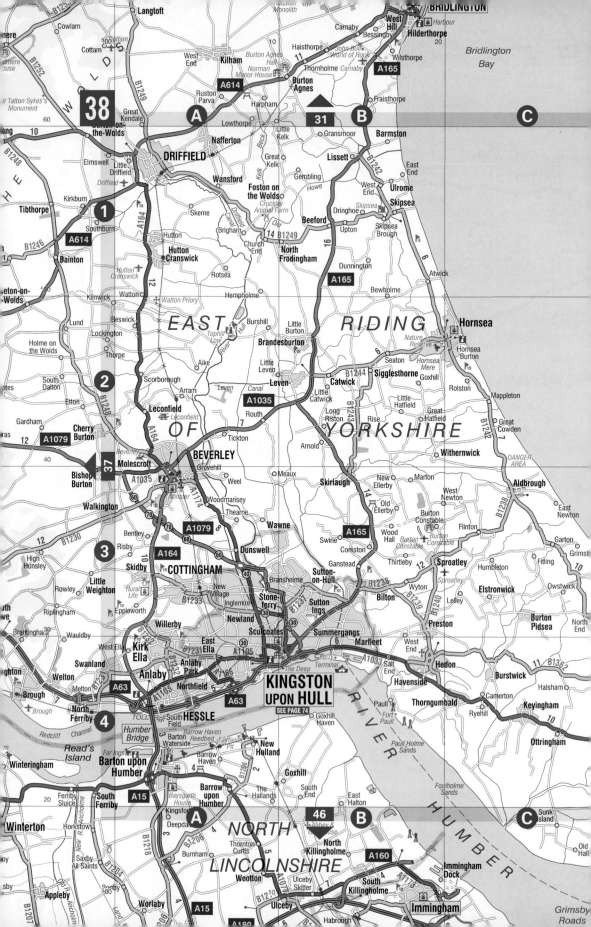

40   ⁵50   60

D   E   F   **39**   60

1   ⁴50

N   O   R   T   H   2   40

S   E   A   3   30

4

20

D   E   **47**   F

40   ⁵50   60

Tunstall

B1242   Waxholme

Rimswell   Owthorne

Withernsea

Hollym

nestead   A1033

Holmpton

Out
Newton

Patrington   Welwick
Haven   B1445   Weeton

D   keffling   **Easington**   E

nk Island
Sands   Kilnsea

*Trinity
Sands*

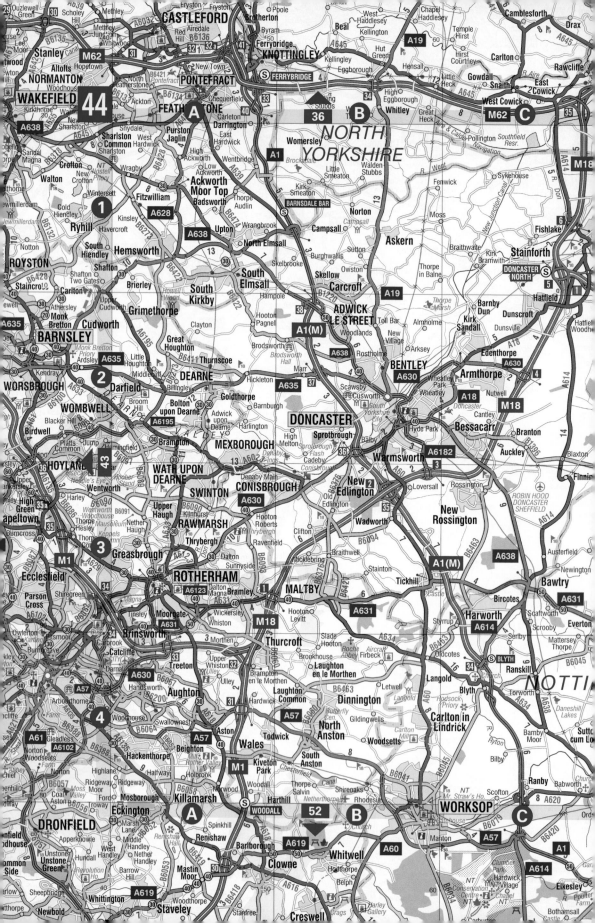

RIDING
YORKSHIRE

Hollym
Holmpton
estead A1033
Patrington
Haven B1445
D
Welwick
Weeton
Out Newton
E
39
F

Skeffling
Easington

nk Island
Sands

Kilnsea

Trinity
Sands

Spurn

1

SPURN
HEAD

10

BY

Mouth

Hull to:
Rotterdam (Europoort) 10hrs.
Zeebrugge 12hrs. 30mins.

CLEETHORPES
Discovery Centre
The Jungle
Cleethorpes Coast
Light Railway
Pleasure Island
Humberston
of

Tetney High Sands

the

Humber

N   O   R   T   H

2

Tetney
Lock
North
Cotes
A1031

Donna Nook
DANGER AREA

400

Marshchapel
Eskham
Churchthorpe
Grainthorpe
Donna Nook

S   E   A

Covenham
Resr.
Fulstow
Grainthorpe Fen
North
Somercotes
DANGER AREA
Skidbrooke
North End

3

colnshire Wolds
Railway
Covenham
St. Bartholomew
Conisholme
Church
End
Saltfleet

Covenham
St. Mary
Utterby
Austin
Fen
South
Somercotes

90

WIRE
Fotherby
Yarburgh
Alvingham
Skidbrooke
Saltfleetby
St. Clements
Saltfleetby-
Theddlethorpe
Dunes

Little
Grimsby
North
Cockerington
A1031
Saltfleetby
All Saints

Keddington
Corner
Saltfleetby
St. Peter
11
Theddlethorpe
St. Helen

Keddington
South
Cockerington
Grimoldby
B1200
Three
Bridges
Theddlethorpe
All Saints
Seal
Sanctuary

LOUTH
Stewton
Manby
Meers
Bridge
Mablethorpe
Ye Olde
Curiosity

4

Manby
Little
Carlton
Great
Carlton

B1520
Legbourne
Little
Cawthorpe
Carlton
South
Reston
12
Gayton
le Marsh
Great
Eau
A1104
Strubby
Thorpe
Trusthorpe
Sutton on Sea

A157
A157
Haugham
Muckton
Authorpe
Tothill
Woodthorpe
B1373
Withern
Strubby
Maltby
le Marsh
Beesby
Sandilands

80

denwell
forth
D
11
Burwell
Belleau
Swaby
Valley
Aby
Claythorpe
Claythorpe Watermill
Wildfowl Gardens
E
55
A1111
Saleby
Markby
Hannah
A52
F

Ruckland
White
Pit
Swaby
Rigsby Wood
Alford
Bilsby
Thurlby
Huttoft
Anderby
Creek

Oxcombe
Ketsby
Calceby
South
Thoresby
Rigsby
Manor House
B1449
13
Anderby
Drainage
Authorpe
Row

Tetford
South
Ormsby
Haugh
Well
Farlesthorpe
A16
15
Mumby
60

Brinkhill
Driby
A1104
Willoughby
Branch Line
Cumberworth

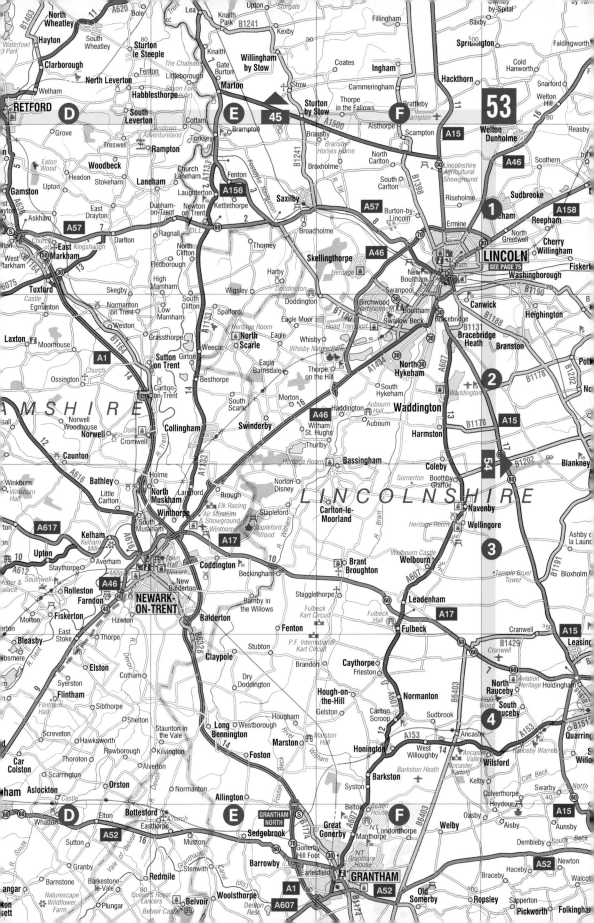

INDEX TO CITIES, TOWNS, VILLAGES, HAMLETS & LOCATIONS

(1) A strict alphabetical order is used e.g. Ashover follows Ash Magna but precedes Ash Parva.

(2) The map reference given refers to the actual map square in which the town spot or built-up area is located and not to the place name.

(3) Where two places of the same name occur in the same County or Unitary Authority, the nearest large town is also given;
e.g. Aisby. *Linc* . . . 3E **45** (nr. Gainsborough) indicates that Aisby is located in square 3E on page **45** and is situated near Gainsborough in the County of Lincolnshire.

COUNTIES AND UNITARY AUTHORITIES with the abbreviations used in this index.

Blackburn with Darwen : *Bkbn*
Blackpool : *Bkpl*
Cheshire : *Ches*
Cumbria : *Cumb*
Darlington : *Darl*
Denbighshire : *Den*
Derby : *Derb*
Derbyshire : *Derbs*
Dumfries & Galloway : *Dum*
Durham : *Dur*
East Riding of Yorkshire : *E Yor*
Flintshire : *Flin*
Greater Manchester : *G Man*
Halton : *Hal*
Hartlepool : *Hart*
Kingston upon Hull : *Hull*
Lancashire : *Lanc*
Leicestershire : *Leics*
Lincolnshire : *Linc*
Merseyside : *Mers*
Middlesbrough : *Midd*
North East Lincolnshire : *NE Lin*
North Lincolnshire : *N Lin*
Northumberland : *Nmbd*
North Yorkshire : *N Yor*
Nottingham : *Nott*
Nottinghamshire : *Notts*
Redcar & Cleveland : *Red C*
Scottish Borders : *Scot*
Shropshire : *Shrp*
South Yorkshire : *S Yor*
Staffordshire : *Staf*
Stockton-on-Tees : *Stoc T*
Stoke-on-Trent : *Stoke*
Tyne & Wear : *Tyne*
Warrington : *Warr*
West Yorkshire : *W Yor*
Wrexham : *Wrex*
York : *York*

A

Abberwick. *Nmbd* . . . 1D **9**
Abbeydale. *S Yor* . . . 4F **43**
Abbeydale Park. *S Yor* . . . 4F **43**
Abbey Hulton. *Stoke* . . . 4B **50**
Abbey St Bathans. *Scot* . . . 1A **4**
Abbeystead. *Lanc* . . . 1D **33**
Abbeytown. *Cumb* . . . 3C **10**
Abbey Village. *Lanc* . . . 4E **33**
Aberford. *W Yor* . . . 3A **36**
Aber-oer. *Wrex* . . . 4A **48**
Abney. *Derbs* . . . 1D **51**
Abram. *G Man* . . . 2E **41**
Aby. *Linc* . . . 1E **55**
Acaster Malbis. *York* . . . 2B **36**
Acaster Selby. *N Yor* . . . 2B **36**
Accrington. *Lanc* . . . 4F **33**
Acklam. *Midd* . . . 3D **21**
Acklam. *N Yor* . . . 4A **30**
Acklington. *Nmbd* . . . 2E **9**
Ackton. *W Yor* . . . 4A **36**
Ackworth Moor Top. *W Yor* . . . 1A **44**
Acomb. *Nmbd* . . . 2E **13**
Acomb. *York* . . . 1B **36**
Acre. *G Man* . . . 2B **42**
Acre. *Lanc* . . . 4F **33**
Acrefair. *Wrex* . . . 4A **48**
Acton. *Ches* . . . 3E **49**
Acton. *Staf* . . . 4A **50**
Acton. *Wrex* . . . 3B **48**
Acton Bridge. *Ches* . . . 1D **49**
Adderley. *Shrp* . . . 4E **49**
Adderstone. *Nmbd* . . . 3D **5**
Addingham. *W Yor* . . . 2C **34**
Addlethorpe. *Linc* . . . 2F **55**
Adlingfleet. *E Yor* . . . 4F **37**
Adlington. *Ches* . . . 4B **42**
Adlington. *Lanc* . . . 1E **41**
Adwalton. *W Yor* . . . 4E **35**
Adwick le Street. *S Yor* . . . 2B **44**
Adwick upon Dearne. *S Yor* . . . 2A **44**
Agglethorpe. *N Yor* . . . 2F **27**
Aglionby. *Cumb* . . . 3F **11**
Aigburth. *Mers* . . . 4B **40**
Aike. *E Yor* . . . 2A **38**
Aiketgate. *Cumb* . . . 4F **11**
Aikhead. *Cumb* . . . 4D **11**
Aikton. *Cumb* . . . 3D **11**
Ainderby Quernhow. *N Yor* . . . 2C **28**
Ainderby Steeple. *N Yor* . . . 1C **28**
Ainsdale. *Mers* . . . 1B **40**
Ainsdale-on-Sea. *Mers* . . . 1A **40**
Ainstable. *Cumb* . . . 4A **12**
Ainsworth. *G Man* . . . 1F **41**
Ainthorpe. *N Yor* . . . 4A **22**
Aintree. *Mers* . . . 3B **40**
Airedale. *W Yor* . . . 4A **36**
Airmyn. *E Yor* . . . 4D **37**
Airton. *N Yor* . . . 1B **34**
Aisby. *Linc* . . . 3E **45** (nr. Gainsborough)
Aisby. *Linc* . . . 4A **54** (nr. Grantham)
Aiskew. *N Yor* . . . 2B **28**
Aislaby. *N Yor* . . . 2A **30** (nr. Pickering)
Aislaby. *N Yor* . . . 4B **22** (nr. Whitby)
Aislaby. *Stoc T* . . . 3D **21**
Aisthorpe. *Linc* . . . 1F **53**
Akeld. *Nmbd* . . . 4B **4**
Albyfield. *Cumb* . . . 3A **12**
Aldborough. *N Yor* . . . 4D **29**
Aldbrough. *E Yor* . . . 3C **38**
Aldbrough St John. *N Yor* . . . 3B **20**
Aldcliffe. *Lanc* . . . 4F **25**
Aldercar. *Derbs* . . . 4A **52**
Alderley Edge. *Ches* . . . 1A **50**
Aldersey Green. *Ches* . . . 3C **48**
Alderwasley. *Derbs* . . . 3F **51**
Aldfield. *N Yor* . . . 4B **28**
Aldford. *Ches* . . . 3C **48**
Aldingham. *Cumb* . . . 3D **25**
Aldoth. *Cumb* . . . 4C **10**
Aldwark. *Derbs* . . . 3E **51**
Aldwark. *N Yor* . . . 4D **29**
Alford. *Linc* . . . 1E **55**
Alfreton. *Derbs* . . . 3A **52**
Algarkirk. *Linc* . . . 4C **54**
Alkborough. *N Lin* . . . 4E **37**
Alkington. *Shrp* . . . 4D **49**
Alkmonton. *Derbs* . . . 4D **51**
Allanton. *Scot* . . . 1A **4**
Allendale Town. *Nmbd* . . . 3D **13**
Allenheads. *Nmbd* . . . 4D **13**
Allensford. *Dur* . . . 4F **13**
Allerby. *Cumb* . . . 1B **16**
Allerston. *N Yor* . . . 2B **30**
Allerthorpe. *E Yor* . . . 2D **37**
Allerton. *Mers* . . . 4C **40**
Allerton. *W Yor* . . . 3D **35**
Allerton Bywater. *W Yor* . . . 4A **36**
Allerton Mauleverer. *N Yor* . . . 1A **36**
Allestree. *Derb* . . . 4F **51**
Allgreave. *Ches* . . . 2B **50**
Allington. *Linc* . . . 4E **53**
Allithwaite. *Cumb* . . . 3E **25**
Allonby. *Cumb* . . . 4B **10**
Alltami. *Flin* . . . 2A **48**
Almholme. *S Yor* . . . 2B **44**
Almington. *Staf* . . . 4F **49**
Almondbury. *W Yor* . . . 1D **43**
Alne. *N Yor* . . . 4D **29**
Alnham. *Nmbd* . . . 1B **8**
Alnmouth. *Nmbd* . . . 1E **9**
Alnwick. *Nmbd* . . . 1D **9**
Alport. *Derbs* . . . 2E **51**
Alpraham. *Ches* . . . 3D **49**
Alsager. *Ches* . . . 3F **49**
Alsagers Bank. *Staf* . . . 4A **50**
Alsop en le Dale. *Derbs* . . . 3D **51**
Alston. *Cumb* . . . 4C **12**
Alstonefield. *Staf* . . . 3D **51**
Altham. *Lanc* . . . 3F **33**
Althorpe. *N Lin* . . . 2E **45**
Altofts. *W Yor* . . . 4F **35**
Alton. *Derbs* . . . 2F **51**
Alton. *Staf* . . . 4C **50**
Altrincham. *G Man* . . . 4F **41**
Alvanley. *Ches* . . . 1C **48**
Alverthorpe. *W Yor* . . . 4F **35**
Alverton. *Notts* . . . 4D **53**
Alvingham. *Linc* . . . 3D **47**
Alwinton. *Nmbd* . . . 2B **8**
Alwoodley. *W Yor* . . . 2E **35**
Ambergate. *Derbs* . . . 3F **51**
Amber Hill. *Linc* . . . 4C **54**
Amble. *Nmbd* . . . 2E **9**
Ambler Thorn. *W Yor* . . . 4C **34**
Ambleside. *Cumb* . . . 4E **17**
Amcotts. *N Lin* . . . 1E **45**
Amisfield. *Dum* . . . 1B **10**
Amotherby. *N Yor* . . . 3A **30**
Ampleforth. *N Yor* . . . 3E **29**
Ampleforth College. *N Yor* . . . 3E **29**
Ancaster. *Linc* . . . 4F **53**
Anchorsholme. *Lanc* . . . 2B **32**
Ancroft. *Nmbd* . . . 2C **4**
Ancrum. *Scot* . . . 1E **7**
Anderby. *Linc* . . . 1F **55**
Anderby Creek. *Linc* . . . 1F **55**
Anderton. *Ches* . . . 1E **49**
Andertons Mill. *Lanc* . . . 1D **41**
Anfield. *Mers* . . . 3B **40**
Angerton. *Cumb* . . . 3D **11**
Angram. *N Yor* . . . 1D **27** (nr. Keld)
Angram. *N Yor* . . . 2B **36** (nr. York)
Anick. *Nmbd* . . . 2E **13**
Ankerbold. *Derbs* . . . 2F **51**
Anlaby. *E Yor* . . . 4A **38**
Anlaby Park. *Hull* . . . 4A **38**
Annan. *Dum* . . . 2C **10**
Annaside. *Cumb* . . . 2B **24**
Annesley. *Notts* . . . 3B **52**
Annesley Woodhouse. *Notts* . . . 3B **52**
Annfield Plain. *Dur* . . . 3A **14**
Ansdell. *Lanc* . . . 4B **32**
Anthorn. *Cumb* . . . 3C **10**
Anton's Gowt. *Linc* . . . 4C **54**
Antrobus. *Ches* . . . 1E **49**
Anwick. *Linc* . . . 3B **54**
Apley. *Linc* . . . 1B **54**
Apperknowle. *Derbs* . . . 1F **51**
Apperley Dene. *Nmbd* . . . 3F **13**
Appersett. *N Yor* . . . 1D **27**
Appleby. *N Lin* . . . 1F **45**
Appleby-in-Westmorland. *Cumb* . . . 2B **18**
Applegarthtown. *Dum* . . . 1C **10**
Applethwaite. *Cumb* . . . 2D **17**
Appleton. *Hal* . . . 1F **41**
Appleton-le-Moors. *N Yor* . . . 2A **30**
Appleton-le-Street. *N Yor* . . . 3A **30**
Appleton Roebuck. *N Yor* . . . 2B **36**
Appleton Thorn. *Warr* . . . 4E **41**
Appleton Wiske. *N Yor* . . . 4C **20**
Appletreehall. *Scot* . . . 1D **7**
Appletreewick. *N Yor* . . . 4F **27**
Appley Bridge. *Lanc* . . . 1D **41**
Arbourthorne. *S Yor* . . . 4F **43**
Archdeacon Newton. *Darl* . . . 3B **20**
Arclid. *Ches* . . . 2F **49**
Arclid Green. *Ches* . . . 2F **49**
Arden Hall. *N Yor* . . . 1E **29**
Ardsley. *S Yor* . . . 2F **43**
Arkendale. *N Yor* . . . 4C **28**
Arkholme. *Lanc* . . . 3A **26**
Arkle Town. *N Yor* . . . 4F **19**
Arksey. *S Yor* . . . 2B **44**
Arkwright Town. *Derbs* . . . 1A **52**
Arlecdon. *Cumb* . . . 3B **16**
Arley. *Ches* . . . 4E **41**
Armathwaite. *Cumb* . . . 4A **12**
Armitage Bridge. *W Yor* . . . 1D **43**
Armley. *W Yor* . . . 3E **35**
Armthorpe. *S Yor* . . . 2C **44**
Arncliffe. *N Yor* . . . 3E **27**
Arncliffe Cote. *N Yor* . . . 3E **27**
Arnold. *E Yor* . . . 2B **38**
Arnold. *Notts* . . . 4B **52**
Arnside. *Cumb* . . . 3F **25**
Arrad Foot. *Cumb* . . . 2E **25**
Arram. *E Yor* . . . 2A **38**
Arras. *E Yor* . . . 2F **37**
Arrathorne. *N Yor* . . . 1B **28**
Arthington. *W Yor* . . . 2E **35**
Asby. *Cumb* . . . 2B **16**
Asenby. *N Yor* . . . 3C **28**
Asgarby. *Linc* . . . 2D **55** (nr. Horncastle)
Asgarby. *Linc* . . . 4B **54** (nr. Sleaford)
Ashbourne. *Derbs* . . . 4D **51**
Ashby. *N Lin* . . . 2E **45**
Ashby by Partney. *Linc* . . . 2E **55**
Ashby cum Fenby. *NE Lin* . . . 2C **46**
Ashby de la Launde. *Linc* . . . 3A **54**
Ashby Puerorum. *Linc* . . . 1D **55**
Ashford in the Water. *Derbs* . . . 2D **51**
Ashington. *Nmbd* . . . 4E **9**
Ashkirk. *Scot* . . . 1C **6**
Ashley. *Ches* . . . 4F **41**
Ashley. *Staf* . . . 4F **49**
Ashley Heath. *Staf* . . . 4F **49**
Ash Magna. *Shrp* . . . 4D **49**
Ashover. *Derbs* . . . 2F **51**
Ash Parva. *Shrp* . . . 4D **49**
Ashton. *Ches* . . . 2D **49**
Ashton-in-Makerfield. *G Man* . . . 2D **41**
Ashton-under-Lyne. *G Man* . . . 3B **42**
Ashton upon Mersey. *G Man* . . . 3F **41**
Ashurst. *Lanc* . . . 2C **40**
Askam in Furness. *Cumb* . . . 3D **25**
Askern. *S Yor* . . . 1B **44**
Askham. *Cumb* . . . 2A **18**
Askham. *Notts* . . . 1D **53**
Askham Bryan. *York* . . . 2B **36**
Askham Richard. *York* . . . 2B **36**
Askrigg. *N Yor* . . . 1E **27**
Askwith. *N Yor* . . . 2D **35**
Aslockton. *Notts* . . . 4D **53**
Aspatria. *Cumb* . . . 4C **10**
Asperton. *Linc* . . . 4C **54**
Aspull. *G Man* . . . 2E **41**
Asselby. *E Yor* . . . 4D **37**
Astbury. *Ches* . . . 2A **50**
Asterby. *Linc* . . . 1C **54**
Astley. *G Man* . . . 2F **41**
Astley Bridge. *G Man* . . . 1F **41**
Aston. *Ches* . . . 1D **49** (nr. Frodsham)
Aston. *Ches* . . . 4E **49** (nr. Nantwich)
Aston. *Derbs* . . . 4D **43**
Aston. *Flin* . . . 2B **48**
Aston. *S Yor* . . . 4A **44**
Aston. *Staf* . . . 4F **49**
Aston juxta Mondrum. *Ches* . . . 3E **49**
Aswarby. *Linc* . . . 4A **54**
Aswardby. *Linc* . . . 1D **55**
Athersley. *S Yor* . . . 2F **43**
Atherton. *G Man* . . . 2E **41**
Atlow. *Derbs* . . . 4E **51**
Attenborough. *Notts* . . . 4B **52**
Atterby. *Linc* . . . 3F **45**
Atwick. *E Yor* . . . 1B **38**
Aubourn. *Linc* . . . 2F **53**
Auchencairn. *Dum* . . . 1A **10**
Auchencrow. *Scot* . . . 1A **4**
Auckley. *S Yor* . . . 2C **44**
Audenshaw. *G Man* . . . 3B **42**
Audlem. *Ches* . . . 4E **49**
Audley. *Staf* . . . 3F **49**
Aughton. *E Yor* . . . 3D **37**
Aughton. *Lanc* . . . 4A **26** (nr. Lancaster)
Aughton. *Lanc* . . . 2B **40** (nr. Ormskirk)
Aughton. *S Yor* . . . 4A **44**
Aughton Park. *Lanc* . . . 2C **40**
Auldgirth. *Dum* . . . 1A **10**
Ault Hucknall. *Derbs* . . . 2A **52**
Aunsby. *Linc* . . . 4A **54**
Austerfield. *S Yor* . . . 3C **44**
Austin Fen. *Linc* . . . 3D **47**
Austwick. *N Yor* . . . 4C **26**
Authorpe. *Linc* . . . 4E **47**
Authorpe Row. *Linc* . . . 1F **55**
Averham. *Notts* . . . 3D **53**
Awsworth. *Notts* . . . 4A **52**
Aycliffe. *Dur* . . . 2B **20**
Aydon. *Nmbd* . . . 2F **13**
Aykley Heads. *Dur* . . . 4B **14**
Ayle. *Nmbd* . . . 4C **12**
Aylesby. *NE Lin* . . . 2C **46**
Aysgarth. *N Yor* . . . 2F **27**
Ayside. *Cumb* . . . 2E **25**
Ayton. *Scot* . . . 1B **4**
Azerley. *N Yor* . . . 3B **28**

B

Babell. *Flin* . . . 1A **48**
Babworth. *Notts* . . . 4C **44**
Backbarrow. *Cumb* . . . 2E **25**
Backford. *Ches* . . . 1C **48**
Backworth. *Tyne* . . . 1C **14**
Bacup. *Lanc* . . . 4A **34**
Baddeley Green. *Stoke* . . . 3B **50**
Badsworth. *W Yor* . . . 1A **44**
Bagby. *N Yor* . . . 2D **29**
Bag Enderby. *Linc* . . . 1D **55**
Bagillt. *Flin* . . . 1A **48**
Bagnall. *Staf* . . . 3B **50**
Bagthorpe. *Notts* . . . 3A **52**
Baildon. *W Yor* . . . 3D **35**
Baildon Green. *W Yor* . . . 3D **35**
Baileyhead. *Cumb* . . . 4D **7**
Bailrigg. *Lanc* . . . 1C **32**
Bainbridge. *N Yor* . . . 1E **27**
Bainton. *E Yor* . . . 1F **37**
Bakewell. *Derbs* . . . 2E **51**
Balby. *S Yor* . . . 2B **44**
Baldersby. *N Yor* . . . 3C **28**
Baldersby St James. *N Yor* . . . 3C **28**
Balderstone. *Lanc* . . . 3E **33**
Balderton. *Ches* . . . 2B **48**
Balderton. *Notts* . . . 3E **53**
Baldwinholme. *Cumb* . . . 3E **11**
Baldwins Gate. *Staf* . . . 4F **49**
Balk. *N Yor* . . . 2D **29**
Balkholme. *E Yor* . . . 4D **37**
Ballidon. *Derbs* . . . 3E **51**
Balterley. *Staf* . . . 3F **49**
Bamber Bridge. *Lanc* . . . 4D **33**
Bamburgh. *Nmbd* . . . 3D **5**
Bamford. *Derbs* . . . 4E **43**
Bampton. *Cumb* . . . 3A **18**
Bampton Grange. *Cumb* . . . 3A **18**
Bangor-is-y-coed. *Wrex* . . . 4B **48**
Bangor's Green. *Lanc* . . . 2B **40**
Bankend. *Dum* . . . 2B **10**
Bank Newton. *N Yor* . . . 1B **34**
Banks. *Cumb* . . . 2A **12**
Banks. *Lanc* . . . 4B **32**
Bankshill. *Dum* . . . 4A **6**
Bank, The. *Ches* . . . 3A **50**
Bank Top. *Lanc* . . . 2D **41**
Barber Booth. *Derbs* . . . 4D **43**
Barber Green. *Cumb* . . . 2E **25**
Barbon. *Cumb* . . . 2B **26**
Barbridge. *Ches* . . . 3E **49**
Barclose. *Cumb* . . . 2F **11**
Barden. *N Yor* . . . 1A **28**
Barden Scale. *N Yor* . . . 1C **34**
Bardney. *Linc* . . . 2B **54**
Bardon Mill. *Nmbd* . . . 2C **12**
Bardsea. *Cumb* . . . 3E **25**
Bardsey. *W Yor* . . . 2F **35**
Bardsley. *G Man* . . . 2B **42**
Bare. *Lanc* . . . 4F **25**
Barelees. *Nmbd* . . . 3A **4**
Barkestone-le-Vale. *Leics* . . . 4D **53**
Barkisland. *W Yor* . . . 1C **42**
Barkston. *Linc* . . . 4F **53**
Barkston Ash. *N Yor* . . . 3A **36**
Barlaston. *Staf* . . . 4A **50**
Barlborough. *Derbs* . . . 1A **52**
Barlby. *N Yor* . . . 3C **36**
Barley. *Lanc* . . . 2A **34**
Barley Mow. *Tyne* . . . 3B **14**
Barlings. *Linc* . . . 1A **54**
Barlow. *Derbs* . . . 1F **51**
Barlow. *N Yor* . . . 4C **36**
Barlow. *Tyne* . . . 2A **14**
Barmby Moor. *E Yor* . . . 2D **37**
Barmby on the Marsh. *E Yor* . . . 4C **36**
Barmoor. *Nmbd* . . . 3C **4**
Barmpton. *Darl* . . . 3C **20**
Barmston. *E Yor* . . . 1B **38**
Barnard Castle. *Dur* . . . 3F **19**
Barnbarroch. *Dum* . . . 3A **10**
Barnburgh. *S Yor* . . . 2A **44**
Barnby Dun. *S Yor* . . . 2C **44**

Barnby in the Willows—Brawby

Barnby in the Willows. *Notts* 3E **53**
Barnby Moor. *Notts* 4C **44**
Barnetby le Wold. *N Lin* 2A **46**
Barningham. *Dur* 3F **19**
Barnoldby le Beck. *NE Lin* 2C **46**
Barnoldswick. *Lanc* 2A **34**
Barnsley. *S Yor* 2F **43**
Barnston. *Mers* 4A **40**
Barnstone. *Notts* 4D **53**
Barnton. *Ches* 1E **49**
Barrasford. *Nmbd* 1E **13**
Barrow. *Lanc* 3F **33**
Barrow Bridge. *G Man* 1E **41**
Barrowburn. *Nmbd* 1A **8**
Barrowby. *Linc* 4E **53**
Barrowcliff. *N Yor* 2D **31**
Barrowford. *Lanc* 3A **34**
Barrow Haven. *N Lin* 4A **38**
Barrow Hill. *Derbs* 1A **52**
Barrow-in-Furness. *Cumb* 4D **25**
Barrow Nook. *Lanc* 2C **40**
Barrow's Green. *Ches* 4D **41**
Barrows Green. *Cumb* 2A **26**
Barrow upon Humber. *N Lin* 4A **38**
Barthomley. *Ches* 3F **49**
Barton. *Ches* 3C **48**
Barton. *Cumb* 2F **17**
Barton. *Lanc* 2B **40** (nr. Ormskirk)
Barton. *Lanc* 3D **33** (nr. Preston)
Barton. *N Yor* 4B **20**
Barton Hill. *N Yor* 4A **30**
Barton-le-Street. *N Yor* 3A **30**
Barton-le-Willows. *N Yor* 4A **30**
Barton-upon-Humber. *N Lin* 4A **38**
Barton Waterside. *N Lin* 4A **38**
Barugh Green. *S Yor* 2F **43**
Barwick in Elmet. *W Yor* 3F **35**
Basford Green. *Staf* 3B **50**
Bashall Eaves. *Lanc* 2E **33**
Bashall Town. *Lanc* 2F **33**
Baslow. *Derbs* 1E **51**
Bassenthwaite. *Cumb* 1D **17**
Bassingfield. *Notts* 4C **52**
Bassingham. *Linc* 2F **53**
Bate Heath. *Ches* 1E **49**
Bathley. *Notts* 3D **53**
Batley. *W Yor* 4E **35**
Battersby. *N Yor* 4E **21**
Baumber. *Linc* 1C **54**
Bawtry. *S Yor* 3C **44**
Baxenden. *Lanc* 4F **33**
Baybridge. *Nmbd* 3E **13**
Baycliff. *Cumb* 3D **25**
Bayles. *Cumb* 4C **12**
Baythorpe. *Linc* 4C **54**
Beadlam. *N Yor* 2F **29**
Beadnell. *Nmbd* 4E **5**
Beal. *Nmbd* 2C **4**
Beal. *N Yor* 4B **36**
Beamhurst. *Staf* 4C **50**
Beamish. *Dur* 3B **14**
Beamsley. *N Yor* 1C **34**
Beanley. *Nmbd* 1C **8**
Beardwood. *Bkbn* 4E **33**
Bearpark. *Dur* 4B **14**
Bearsbridge. *Nmbd* 3C **12**
Bearstone. *Shrp* 4F **49**
Beauchief. *S Yor* 4F **43**
Beaumont. *Cumb* 3E **11**
Beaumont Hill. *Darl* 3B **20**
Beauvale. *Notts* 4A **52**
Bebington. *Mers* 4B **40**
Bebside. *Nmbd* 4E **9**
Becconsall. *Lanc* 4C **32**
Beckermet. *Cumb* 4B **16**
Beckfoot. *Cumb* 2C **24** (nr. Broughton in Furness)
Beck Foot. *Cumb* 1B **26** (nr. Kendal)
Beckfoot. *Cumb* 4C **16** (nr. Seascale)
Beckfoot. *Cumb* 4B **10** (nr. Silloth)
Beck Hole. *N Yor* 4B **22**
Beckingham. *Linc* 3E **53**
Beckingham. *Notts* 3D **45**
Beck Side. *Cumb* 2E **25** (nr. Cartmel)
Beckside. *Cumb* 2B **26** (nr. Sedbergh)
Beck Side. *Cumb* 2D **25** (nr. Ulverston)
Beckwithshaw. *N Yor* 1E **35**
Bedale. *N Yor* 2B **28**
Bedburn. *Dur* 1A **20**
Bedford. *G Man* 2E **41**
Bedlam. *N Yor* 4B **28**
Bedlington. *Nmbd* 4E **9**
Bedrule. *Scot* 1E **7**
Beech. *Staf* 4A **50**
Beechcliffe. *W Yor* 2C **34**
Beeford. *E Yor* 1B **38**
Beeley. *Derbs* 2E **51**
Beelsby. *NE Lin* 2C **46**
Beesby. *Linc* 1E **55**
Beeston. *Ches* 3D **49**
Beeston. *Notts* 4B **52**
Beeston. *W Yor* 3E **35**
Beeswing. *Dum* 2A **10**
Beetham. *Cumb* 3F **25**
Beighton. *S Yor* 4A **44**
Beighton Hill. *Derbs* 3E **51**
Belchford. *Linc* 1C **54**
Belford. *Nmbd* 3D **5**
Bell Busk. *N Yor* 1B **34**
Belleau. *Linc* 1E **55**
Bellerby. *N Yor* 1A **28**
Bellerby Camp. *N Yor* 1F **27**
Belle Vue. *Cumb* 1C **16**
Bellingham. *Nmbd* 4A **8**
Bellshill. *Nmbd* 3D **5**
Belmont. *Bkbn* 1E **41**
Belper. *Derbs* 4F **51**
Belper Lane End. *Derbs* 4F **51**
Belph. *Derbs* 1B **52**
Belsay. *Nmbd* 1A **14**
Belthorn. *Lanc* 4F **33**
Beltoft. *N Lin* 2E **45**
Belton. *Linc* 4F **53**
Belton. *N Lin* 2D **45**
Belvoir. *Leics* 4E **53**
Bempton. *E Yor* 3E **31**
Benchill. *G Man* 4A **42**
Benfieldside. *Dur* 3F **13**
Benington. *Linc* 4D **55**
Benington Sea End. *Linc* 4E **55**
Bennethead. *Cumb* 2F **17**
Benningbrough. *N Yor* 1B **36**
Benniworth. *Linc* 4C **46**
Benthall. *Nmbd* 4E **5**
Bentley. *E Yor* 3A **38**
Bentley. *S Yor* 2B **44**
Bentpath. *Dum* 3B **6**
Benwell. *Tyne* 2B **14**
Berrier. *Cumb* 2F **17**
Berrington. *Nmbd* 2C **4**
Berrington Law. *Nmbd* 2B **4**
Berryscaur. *Dum* 3A **6**
Bersham. *Wrex* 4B **48**
Berwick Hill. *Nmbd* 1A **14**
Berwick-upon-Tweed. *Nmbd* 1C **4**
Berwyn. *Den* 4A **48**
Bescar. *Lanc* 1B **40**
Bessacarr. *S Yor* 2C **44**
Bessingby. *E Yor* 4E **31**
Besthorpe. *Notts* 2E **53**
Bestwood Village. *Notts* 4B **52**
Beswick. *E Yor* 2A **38**
Betley. *Staf* 4F **49**
Bettisfield. *Wrex* 4C **48**
Betton. *Shrp* 4E **49**
Bevercotes. *Notts* 1C **52**
Beverley. *E Yor* 3A **38**
Bewaldeth. *Cumb* 1D **17**
Bewcastle. *Cumb* 1A **12**
Bewerley. *N Yor* 4A **28**
Bewholme. *E Yor* 2B **38**
Bibbington. *Derbs* 1C **50**
Bicker. *Linc* 4C **54**
Bicker Bar. *Linc* 4C **54**
Bicker Gauntlet. *Linc* 4C **54**
Bickershaw. *G Man* 2E **41**
Bickerstaffe. *Lanc* 2C **40**
Bickerton. *Ches* 3D **49**
Bickerton. *Nmbd* 2B **8**
Bickerton. *N Yor* 1A **36**
Bickley. *N Yor* 1C **30**
Bickley Moss. *Ches* 4D **49**
Biddlestone. *Nmbd* 2B **8**
Biddulph. *Staf* 3A **50**
Biddulph Moor. *Staf* 3B **50**
Bidston. *Mers* 4A **40**
Bielby. *E Yor* 2D **37**
Bierley. *W Yor* 3D **35**
Bigby. *Linc* 2A **46**
Biggar. *Cumb* 4C **24**
Biggin. *Derbs* 3D **51** (nr. Hartington)
Biggin. *Derbs* 4E **51** (nr. Hulland)
Biggin. *N Yor* 3B **36**
Biglands. *Cumb* 3D **11**
Bilborough. *Nott* 4B **52**
Bilbrough. *N Yor* 2B **36**
Bilby. *Notts* 4C **44**
Bildershaw. *Dur* 2B **20**
Billingborough. *Linc* 4B **54**
Billinge. *Mers* 2D **41**
Billingham. *Stoc T* 2D **21**
Billinghay. *Linc* 3B **54**
Billingley. *S Yor* 2A **44**
Billington. *Lanc* 3F **33**
Billy Row. *Dur* 1A **20**
Bilsborrow. *Lanc* 2D **33**
Bilsby. *Linc* 1E **55**
Bilsthorpe. *Notts* 2C **52**
Bilsthorpe Moor. *Notts* 3C **52**
Bilton. *E Yor* 3B **38**
Bilton. *Nmbd* 1E **9**
Bilton. *N Yor* 1E **35** (nr. Harrogate)
Bilton. *N Yor* 2A **36** (nr. York)
Binbrook. *Linc* 3C **46**
Binchester Blocks. *Dur* 1B **20**
Bingfield. *Nmbd* 1E **13**
Bingham. *Notts* 4D **53**
Bingley. *W Yor* 3D **35**
Binsoe. *N Yor* 3B **28**
Birchall. *Staf* 3B **50**
Birch Heath. *Ches* 2D **49**
Birch Hill. *Ches* 1D **49**
Birch Langley. *G Man* 2A **42**
Birchover. *Derbs* 2E **51**
Birch Vale. *Derbs* 4C **42**
Birchwood. *Linc* 2F **53**
Birchwood. *Warr* 3E **41**
Bircotes. *Notts* 3C **44**
Birdsall. *N Yor* 4B **30**
Birds Edge. *W Yor* 2E **43**
Birdwell. *S Yor* 2F **43**
Birgham. *Scot* 3A **4**
Birkby. *Cumb* 1B **16**
Birkby. *N Yor* 4C **20**
Birkdale. *Mers* 1B **40**
Birkenhead. *Mers* 4B **40**
Birkenshaw. *W Yor* 4E **35**
Birkin. *N Yor* 4B **36**
Birling. *Nmbd* 2E **9**
Birstall Smithies. *W Yor* 4E **35**
Birstwith. *N Yor* 1E **35**
Birthorpe. *Linc* 4B **54**
Birtle. *Lanc* 1A **42**
Birtley. *Nmbd* 1D **13**
Birtley. *Tyne* 3B **14**
Bishop Auckland. *Dur* 2B **20**
Bishopbridge. *Linc* 3A **46**
Bishop Burton. *E Yor* 3F **37**
Bishop Middleham. *Dur* 1C **20**
Bishop Monkton. *N Yor* 4C **28**
Bishop Norton. *Linc* 3F **45**
Bishop Thornton. *N Yor* 4B **28**
Bishopthorpe. *York* 2B **36**
Bishopton. *Darl* 2C **20**
Bishopton. *N Yor* 3C **28**
Bishop Wilton. *E Yor* 1D **37**
Bispham. *Bkpl* 2B **32**
Bispham Green. *Lanc* 1C **40**
Blackbrook. *Derbs* 4F **51**
Blackbrook. *Mers* 3D **41**
Blackbrook. *Staf* 4F **49**
Blackburn. *Bkbn* 4E **33**
Black Callerton. *Tyne* 2A **14**
Blackden Heath. *Ches* 1F **49**
Blackdyke. *Cumb* 3C **10**
Blacker Hill. *S Yor* 2F **43**
Blackford. *Cumb* 2E **11**
Blackhall Colliery. *Dur* 1D **21**
Blackhall Mill. *Tyne* 3A **14**
Blackhall Rocks. *Dur* 1D **21**
Black Heddon. *Nmbd* 1F **13**
Blackjack. *Linc* 4C **54**
Black Lane. *G Man* 2F **41**
Blackleach. *Lanc* 3C **32**
Blackley. *G Man* 2A **42**
Blackley. *W Yor* 4D **35**
Blackmoor. *G Man* 2E **41**
Blacko. *Lanc* 2A **34**
Blackpool. *Bkpl* 3B **32**
Blackpool Airport. *Lanc* 3B **32**
Blackpool Gate. *Cumb* 1A **12**
Blackrod. *G Man* 1E **41**
Blackshaw. *Dum* 2B **10**
Blackshaw Head. *W Yor* 4B **34**
Blacksnape. *Bkbn* 4F **33**
Blacktoft. *E Yor* 4E **37**
Blackwell. *Darl* 3B **20**
Blackwell. *Derbs* 3A **52** (nr. Alfreton)
Blackwell. *Derbs* 1D **51** (nr. Buxton)
Blackwood Hill. *Staf* 3B **50**
Blacon. *Ches* 2B **48**
Blagill. *Nmbd* 4C **12**
Blaguegate. *Lanc* 2C **40**
Blakenhall. *Ches* 4F **49**
Blanchland. *Nmbd* 3E **13**
Bland Hill. *N Yor* 1E **35**
Blankney. *Linc* 2A **54**
Blawith. *Cumb* 2D **25**
Blaxton. *S Yor* 2C **44**
Blaydon. *Tyne* 2A **14**
Bleasby. *Linc* 4B **46**
Bleasby. *Notts* 4D **53**
Bleasby Moor. *Linc* 4B **46**
Blencarn. *Cumb* 1B **18**
Blencogo. *Cumb* 4C **10**
Blennerhasset. *Cumb* 4C **10**
Bletchley. *Shrp* 4E **49**
Blidworth. *Notts* 3B **52**
Blindburn. *Nmbd* 1A **8**
Blindcrake. *Cumb* 1C **16**
Blitterlees. *Cumb* 3C **10**
Bloomfield. *Scot* 1D **7**
Blore. *Staf* 4D **51**
Bloxholm. *Linc* 3A **54**
Blubberhouses. *N Yor* 1D **35**
Blurton. *Stoke* 4A **50**
Blyborough. *Linc* 3F **45**
Blyth. *Nmbd* 4F **9**
Blyth. *Notts* 4C **44**
Blythe Bridge. *Staf* 4B **50**
Blythe Marsh. *Staf* 4B **50**
Blyton. *Linc* 3E **45**
Boar's Head. *G Man* 2D **41**
Bolam. *Dur* 2A **20**
Bolam. *Nmbd* 4C **8**
Bold Heath. *Mers* 4D **41**
Boldon. *Tyne* 2C **14**
Boldon Colliery. *Tyne* 2C **14**
Boldron. *Dur* 3F **19**
Bole. *Notts* 4D **45**
Bolehill. *Derbs* 3E **51**
Bollington. *Ches* 1B **50**
Bolsover. *Derbs* 1A **52**
Bolsterstone. *S Yor* 3E **43**
Boltby. *N Yor* 2D **29**
Bolton. *Cumb* 2B **18**
Bolton. *E Yor* 1D **37**
Bolton. *G Man* 2F **41**
Bolton. *Nmbd* 1D **9**
Bolton Abbey. *N Yor* 1C **34**
Bolton by Bowland. *Lanc* 2F **33**
Boltonfellend. *Cumb* 2F **11**
Boltongate. *Cumb* 4D **11**
Bolton Green. *Lanc* 1D **41**
Bolton-le-Sands. *Lanc* 4F **25**
Bolton Low Houses. *Cumb* 4D **11**
Bolton New Houses. *Cumb* 4D **11**
Bolton-on-Swale. *N Yor* 1B **28**
Bolton Percy. *N Yor* 2B **36**
Bolton Town End. *Lanc* 4F **25**
Bolton upon Dearne. *S Yor* 2A **44**
Bolton Wood Lane. *Cumb* 4D **11**
Bomarsund. *Nmbd* 4E **9**
Bonby. *N Lin* 1A **46**
Bonchester Bridge. *Scot* 1D **7**
Bonds. *Lanc* 2C **32**
Bonjedward. *Scot* 1E **7**
Bonsall. *Derbs* 3E **51**
Bonthorpe. *Linc* 1E **55**
Boosbeck. *Red C* 3F **21**
Boot. *Cumb* 4C **16**
Booth. *W Yor* 4C **34**
Boothby Graffoe. *Linc* 3F **53**
Booth Green. *Ches* 4B **42**
Boothstown. *G Man* 2F **41**
Booth Wood. *W Yor* 1C **42**
Bootle. *Cumb* 2C **24**
Bootle. *Mers* 3B **40**
Booze. *N Yor* 4F **19**
Bordley. *N Yor* 4E **27**
Boreland. *Dum* 3A **6**
Boroughbridge. *N Yor* 4C **28**
Borras Head. *Wrex* 3B **48**
Borrowash. *Derbs* 4F **51**
Borrowby. *N Yor* 2D **29** (nr. Northallerton)
Borrowby. *N Yor* 3A **22** (nr. Whitby)
Borwick. *Lanc* 3A **26**
Bosley. *Ches* 2B **50**
Bossall. *N Yor* 4A **30**
Bostock Green. *Ches* 2E **49**
Boston. *Linc* 4D **55**
Boston Spa. *W Yor* 2A **36**
Bothal. *Nmbd* 4E **9**
Bothamsall. *Notts* 1C **52**
Bothel. *Cumb* 1C **16**
Bottesford. *Leics* 4E **53**
Bottesford. *N Lin* 2E **45**
Bottom o' th' Moor. *G Man* 1E **41**
Botton Head. *Lanc* 4B **26**
Boughton. *Notts* 2C **52**
Boulby. *Red C* 3A **22**
Boulmer. *Nmbd* 1E **9**
Boultham. *Linc* 2F **53**
Boundary. *Staf* 4B **50**
Bournmoor. *Dur* 3C **14**
Boustead Hill. *Cumb* 3D **11**
Bouth. *Cumb* 2E **25**
Bouthwaite. *N Yor* 3A **28**
Bowbank. *Dur* 2E **19**
Bowburn. *Dur* 1C **20**
Bowdon. *G Man* 4F **41**
Bower. *Nmbd* 4F **7**
Bowers. *Staf* 4A **50**
Bowes. *Dur* 3E **19**
Bowgreave. *Lanc* 2C **32**
Bowland Bridge. *Cumb* 2F **25**
Bowlees. *Dur* 2E **19**
Bowling. *W Yor* 3D **35**
Bowling Bank. *Wrex* 4C **48**
Bowmanstead. *Cumb* 1E **25**
Bowness-on-Solway. *Cumb* 2D **11**
Bowness-on-Windermere. *Cumb* 1F **25**
Bowscale. *Cumb* 1E **17**
Bowsden. *Nmbd* 2B **4**
Bowston. *Cumb* 1F **25**
Boylestone. *Derbs* 4D **51**
Boylestonfield. *Derbs* 4D **51**
Boynton. *E Yor* 4E **31**
Boythorpe. *Derbs* 2F **51**
Bracebridge. *Linc* 2F **53**
Bracebridge Heath. *Linc* 2F **53**
Braceby. *Linc* 4A **54**
Bracewell. *Lanc* 2A **34**
Brackenfield. *Derbs* 3F **51**
Brackenlands. *Cumb* 4D **11**
Brackenthwaite. *Cumb* 4D **11**
Brackenthwaite. *N Yor* 1E **35**
Bracon. *N Lin* 2D **45**
Bradbourne. *Derbs* 3E **51**
Bradbury. *Dur* 2C **20**
Bradfield Green. *Ches* 3E **49**
Bradford. *Derbs* 2E **51**
Bradford. *Nmbd* 3D **5**
Bradford. *W Yor* 3D **35**
Bradley. *Ches* 1D **49**
Bradley. *Derbs* 4E **51**
Bradley. *NE Lin* 2C **46**
Bradley. *N Yor* 2F **27**
Bradley. *W Yor* 4D **35**
Bradley. *Wrex* 3B **48**
Bradley Green. *Ches* 4D **49**
Bradley in the Moors. *Staf* 4C **50**
Bradley Mount. *Ches* 1B **50**
Bradnop. *Staf* 3C **50**
Bradshaw. *G Man* 1F **41**
Bradwall Green. *Ches* 2F **49**
Bradway. *S Yor* 1F **51**
Bradwell. *Derbs* 4D **43**
Brafferton. *Darl* 2B **20**
Brafferton. *N Yor* 3D **29**
Braides. *Lanc* 1C **32**
Brailsford. *Derbs* 4E **51**
Braithwaite. *Cumb* 2D **17**
Braithwaite. *S Yor* 1C **44**
Braithwaite. *W Yor* 2C **34**
Braithwell. *S Yor* 3B **44**
Bramcote. *Notts* 4B **52**
Bramhall. *G Man* 4A **42**
Bramham. *W Yor* 2A **36**
Bramhope. *W Yor* 2E **35**
Bramley. *S Yor* 3A **44**
Bramley. *W Yor* 3E **35**
Bramley Head. *N Yor* 1D **35**
Bramley Vale. *Derbs* 2A **52**
Brampton. *Cumb* 2B **18** (nr. Appleby)
Brampton. *Cumb* 2A **12** (nr. Carlisle)
Brampton. *Linc* 1E **53**
Brampton. *S Yor* 2A **44**
Brampton en le Morthen. *S Yor* 4A **44**
Bramshall. *Staf* 4C **50**
Brancepeth. *Dur* 1B **20**
Branch End. *Nmbd* 2F **13**
Brand End. *Linc* 4D **55**
Brandesburton. *E Yor* 2B **38**
Brandon. *Dur* 1B **20**
Brandon. *Linc* 4F **53**
Brandon. *Nmbd* 1C **8**
Brandsby. *N Yor* 3E **29**
Brandy Wharf. *Linc* 3A **46**
Bransby. *Linc* 1F **53**
Bransholme. *Hull* 3A **38**
Branston. *Linc* 2A **54**
Branston Booths. *Linc* 2A **54**
Bransty. *Cumb* 3A **16**
Brant Broughton. *Linc* 3F **53**
Branthwaite. *Cumb* 1D **17** (nr. Caldbeck)
Branthwaite. *Cumb* 2B **16** (nr. Workington)
Brantingham. *E Yor* 4F **37**
Branton. *Nmbd* 1C **8**
Branton. *S Yor* 2C **44**
Branton Green. *N Yor* 4D **29**
Branxholme. *Scot* 1C **6**
Branxton. *Nmbd* 3A **4**
Brassington. *Derbs* 3E **51**
Bratoft. *Linc* 2E **55**
Brattleby. *Linc* 4F **45**
Brawby. *N Yor* 3A **30**

Fishburn—Haisthorpe

Fishburn. *Dur* 1C **20**
Fisher's Row. *Lanc* 2C **32**
Fishlake. *S Yor* 1C **44**
Fishpool. *G Man* 2A **42**
Fishtoft. *Linc* 4D **55**
Fishtoft Drove. *Linc* 4D **55**
Fishwick. *Scot* 1B **4**
Fiskerton. *Linc* 1A **54**
Fiskerton. *Notts* 3D **53**
Fitling. *E Yor* 3C **38**
Fitzwilliam. *W Yor* 1A **44**
Five Lane Ends. *Lanc* 1D **33**
Flagg. *Derbs* 2D **51**
Flamborough. *E Yor* 3F **31**
Flasby. *N Yor* 1B **34**
Flash. *Staf* 2C **50**
Flatt, The. *Cumb* 1A **12**
Flawborough. *Notts* 4D **53**
Flawith. *N Yor* 4D **29**
Flaxby. *N Yor* 1F **35**
Flaxholme. *Derbs* 4F **51**
Flaxton. *N Yor* 4F **29**
Fledborough. *Notts* 1E **53**
Fleetwood. *Lanc* 2B **32**
Fletchertown. *Cumb* 4D **11**
Flimby. *Cumb* 1B **16**
Flint. *Flin* 1A **48**
Flintham. *Notts* 4D **53**
Flint Mountain. *Flin* 1A **48**
Flinton. *E Yor* 3C **38**
Flixborough. *N Lin* 1E **45**
Flixton. *G Man* 3F **41**
Flixton. *N Yor* 3D **31**
Flockton. *W Yor* 1E **43**
Flodden. *Nmbd* 3B **4**
Flookburgh. *Cumb* 3E **25**
Flotterton. *Nmbd* 2C **8**
Flyde, The. *Lanc* 3C **32**
Fockerby. *N Lin* 1E **45**
Foggathorpe. *E Yor* 3D **37**
Fogo. *Scot* 2A **4**
Fogorig. *Scot* 2A **4**
Fole. *Staf* 4C **50**
Folkingham. *Linc* 4A **54**
Folkton. *N Yor* 3D **31**
Follifoot. *N Yor* 1F **35**
Foolow. *Derbs* 1D **51**
Force Forge. *Cumb* 1E **25**
Force Mills. *Cumb* 1E **25**
Forcett. *N Yor* 3A **20**
Ford. *Derbs* 1A **52**
Ford. *Nmbd* 3B **4**
Ford. *Staf* 3C **50**
Ford Green. *Lanc* 2C **32**
Fordington. *Linc* 1E **55**
Fordon. *E Yor* 3D **31**
Forest. *N Yor* 4B **20**
Forestburn Gate. *Nmbd* 3C **8**
Forest Hall. *Cumb* 4A **18**
Forest Head. *Cumb* 3A **12**
Forest-in-Teesdale. *Dur* 2D **19**
Forest Town. *Notts* 2B **52**
Formby. *Mers* 2A **40**
Forsbrook. *Staf* 4B **50**
Forton. *Lanc* 1C **32**
Foston. *Linc* 4E **53**
Foston. *N Yor* 4F **29**
Foston on the Wolds. *E Yor* 1B **38**
Fotherby. *Linc* 3D **47**
Fothergill. *Cumb* 1B **16**
Foulbridge. *Cumb* 4F **11**
Foulden. *Scot* 1B **4**
Foulridge. *Lanc* 2A **34**
Four Lane End. *S Yor* 2E **43**
Four Lane Ends. *Lanc* 2B **32** (nr. Blackpool)
Four Lane Ends. *Lanc* 1D **33** (nr. Lancaster)
Fourlanes End. *Ches* 3A **50**
Fourstones. *Nmbd* 2D **13**
Fowley Common. *Warr* 3E **41**
Foxfield. *Cumb* 2D **25**
Foxholes. *N Yor* 3D **31**
Foxt. *Staf* 4C **50**
Foxton. *Dur* 2C **20**
Foxton. *N Yor* 1D **29**
Foxup. *N Yor* 3D **27**
Foxwist Green. *Ches* 2E **49**
Fraisthorpe. *E Yor* 4E **31**
Frampton. *Linc* 4D **55**
Frampton West End. *Linc* 4C **54**
Framwellgate Moor. *Dur* 4B **14**
Frandley. *Ches* 1E **49**
Frankby. *Mers* 4A **40**
Freckleton. *Lanc* 4C **32**
Freiston. *Linc* 4D **55**
Freiston Shore. *Linc* 4D **55**
Fremington. *N Yor* 1F **27**
Freshfield. *Mers* 2A **40**
Fridaythorpe. *E Yor* 1E **37**
Friden. *Derbs* 2D **51**
Friesthorpe. *Linc* 4A **46**
Frieston. *Linc* 4F **53**
Friezeland. *Notts* 3A **52**
Frisby. *Linc* 2E **55**
Friskney. *Linc* 3E **55**
Friskney Eaudyke. *Linc* 3E **55**
Fritchley. *Derbs* 3F **51**
Frith Bank. *Linc* 4D **55**
Frithville. *Linc* 3D **55**
Frizinghall. *W Yor* 3D **35**
Frizington. *Cumb* 3B **16**
Frodingham. *N Lin* 1F **45**
Frodsham. *Ches* 1D **49**
Froggat. *Derbs* 1E **51**
Froghall. *Staf* 4C **50**
Froncysyllte. *Den* 4A **48**
Fron Isaf. *Wrex* 4A **48**
Frosterley. *Dur* 1F **19**
Fryton. *N Yor* 3F **29**
Fulbeck. *Linc* 3F **53**
Fulford. *Staf* 4B **50**
Fulford. *York* 2C **36**
Fuller's Moor. *Ches* 3C **48**
Fulletby. *Linc* 1C **54**
Full Sutton. *E Yor* 1D **37**
Fulnetby. *Linc* 1B **54**
Fulstow. *Linc* 3D **47**
Fulthorpe. *Stoc T* 2D **21**
Fulwell. *Tyne* 3C **14**
Fulwood. *Lanc* 3D **33**
Fulwood. *Notts* 3A **52**
Fulwood. *S Yor* 4E **43**
Furness Vale. *Derbs* 4C **42**
Fylingthorpe. *N Yor* 4C **22**

G

Gainford. *Dur* 3A **20**
Gainsborough. *Linc* 3E **45**
Gaisgill. *Cumb* 4B **18**
Gaitsgill. *Cumb* 4E **11**
Galgate. *Lanc* 1C **32**
Gallows Green. *Staf* 4C **50**
Galphay. *N Yor* 3B **28**
Gamblesby. *Cumb* 1B **18**
Gamelsby. *Cumb* 3D **11**
Gamesley. *Derbs* 3C **42**
Gammersgill. *N Yor* 2F **27**
Gamston. *Notts* 1D **53** (nr. East Retford)
Gamston. *Notts* 4C **52** (nr. Nottingham)
Ganstead. *E Yor* 3B **38**
Ganthorpe. *N Yor* 3F **29**
Ganton. *N Yor* 3C **30**
Garden City. *Flin* 2B **48**
Garden Village. *S Yor* 3E **43**
Garden Village. *W Yor* 3A **36**
Gardham. *E Yor* 2F **37**
Garforth. *W Yor* 3A **36**
Gargrave. *N Yor* 1B **34**
Garmondsway. *Dur* 1C **20**
Garnett Bridge. *Cumb* 1A **26**
Garrigill. *Cumb* 4C **12**
Garriston. *N Yor* 1A **28**
Garsdale. *Cumb* 2C **26**
Garsdale Head. *Cumb* 1C **26**
Garshall Green. *Staf* 4B **50**
Garstang. *Lanc* 2C **32**
Garston. *Mers* 4C **40**
Garswood. *Mers* 3D **41**
Garth. *Den* 4A **48**
Garthorpe. *N Lin* 1E **45**
Garth Row. *Cumb* 1A **26**
Garton. *E Yor* 3C **38**
Garton-on-the-Wolds. *E Yor* 1F **37**
Garwick. *Linc* 4B **54**
Gateacre. *Mers* 4C **40**
Gatebeck. *Cumb* 2A **26**
Gate Burton. *Linc* 4E **45**
Gateforth. *N Yor* 4B **36**
Gate Helmsley. *N Yor* 1C **36**
Gatehouse. *Nmbd* 4F **7**
Gatenby. *N Yor* 2C **28**
Gatesgarth. *Cumb* 3C **16**
Gateshead. *Tyne* 2B **14**
Gatesheath. *Ches* 2C **48**
Gathurst. *G Man* 2D **41**
Gatley. *G Man* 4A **42**
Gautby. *Linc* 1B **54**
Gavinton. *Scot* 1A **4**
Gawber. *S Yor* 2F **43**
Gawsworth. *Ches* 2A **50**
Gawthorpe. *W Yor* 4E **35**
Gawthrop. *Cumb* 2B **26**
Gawthwaite. *Cumb* 2D **25**
Gayle. *N Yor* 2D **27**
Gayles. *N Yor* 4A **20**
Gayton. *Mers* 4A **40**
Gayton le Marsh. *Linc* 4E **47**
Gayton le Wold. *Linc* 4C **46**
Gedling. *Notts* 4C **52**
Gee Cross. *G Man* 3B **42**
Gelston. *Linc* 4F **53**
Gembling. *E Yor* 1B **38**
Gerrard's Bromley. *Staf* 4F **49**
Gibraltar. *Linc* 3F **55**
Gibsmere. *Notts* 4D **53**
Giggleswick. *N Yor* 4D **27**
Gilberdyke. *E Yor* 4E **37**
Gilcrux. *Cumb* 1C **16**
Gildersome. *W Yor* 4E **35**
Gildingwells. *S Yor* 4B **44**
Gilesgate Moor. *Dur* 4B **14**
Gillamoor. *N Yor* 2F **29**
Gillar's Green. *Mers* 3C **40**
Gilling East. *N Yor* 3F **29**
Gilling West. *N Yor* 4A **20**
Gillow Heath. *Staf* 3A **50**
Gilmanscleuch. *Scot* 1B **6**
Gilmonby. *Dur* 3E **19**
Gilsland. *Nmbd* 2B **12**
Gilsland Spa. *Cumb* 2B **12**
Giltbrook. *Notts* 4A **52**
Gipsey Bridge. *Linc* 4C **54**
Gipton. *W Yor* 3F **35**
Girsby. *N Yor* 4C **20**
Girton. *Notts* 2E **53**
Gisburn. *Lanc* 2A **34**
Glaisdale. *N Yor* 4A **22**
Glanton. *Nmbd* 1C **8**
Glanton Pyke. *Nmbd* 1C **8**
Glan-y-don. *Flin* 1A **48**
Glapwell. *Derbs* 2A **52**
Glasshouses. *N Yor* 4A **28**
Glasson. *Cumb* 2D **11**
Glasson. *Lanc* 1C **32**
Glassonby. *Cumb* 1A **18**
Glazebrook. *Warr* 3E **41**
Glazebury. *Warr* 3E **41**
Gleadless. *S Yor* 4F **43**
Gleadsmoss. *Ches* 2A **50**
Gleaston. *Cumb* 3D **25**
Gledrid. *Shrp* 4A **48**
Glencaple. *Dum* 2A **10**
Glenesslin. *Dum* 1A **10**
Glenkerry. *Scot* 1A **6**
Glenkiln. *Dum* 1A **10**
Glenridding. *Cumb* 3E **17**
Glentham. *Linc* 3A **46**
Glentworth. *Linc* 4F **45**
Glenzierfoot. *Dum* 1E **11**
Glossop. *Derbs* 3C **42**
Gloster Hill. *Nmbd* 2E **9**
Glusburn. *N Yor* 2C **34**
Glutton Bridge. *Staf* 2C **50**
Glyn Ceiriog. *Wrex* 4A **48**
Glyndyfrdwy. *Den* 4A **48**
Goathland. *N Yor* 4B **22**
Gobowen. *Shrp* 4B **48**
Godleybrook. *Staf* 4B **50**
Godstone. *Staf* 4C **50**
Golborne. *G Man* 3E **41**
Golcar. *W Yor* 1C **42**
Golden Grove. *N Yor* 4B **22**
Goldenhill. *Stoke* 3A **50**
Goldsborough. *N Yor* 1F **35** (nr. Harrogate)
Goldsborough. *N Yor* 3B **22** (nr. Whitby)
Goldthorpe. *S Yor* 2A **44**
Gollinglith Foot. *N Yor* 2A **28**
Gomersal. *W Yor* 4E **35**
Gonalston. *Notts* 4C **52**
Gonerby Hill Foot. *Linc* 4F **53**
Goodmanham. *E Yor* 2E **37**
Goodshaw. *Lanc* 4A **34**
Goodshaw Fold. *Lanc* 4A **34**
Goole. *E Yor* 4D **37**
Goose Green. *Cumb* 2A **26**
Goosnargh. *Lanc* 3D **33**
Goostrey. *Ches* 2F **49**
Gorsedd. *Flin* 1A **48**
Gorseybank. *Derbs* 3E **51**
Gorstella. *Ches* 2B **48**
Gorton. *G Man* 3A **42**
Gosforth. *Cumb* 4B **16**
Gosforth. *Tyne* 2B **14**
Goswick. *Nmbd* 2C **4**
Goulceby. *Linc* 1C **54**
Goverton. *Notts* 3D **53**
Gowdall. *E Yor* 4C **36**
Gowthorpe. *E Yor* 1D **37**
Goxhill. *E Yor* 2B **38**
Goxhill. *N Lin* 4B **38**
Goxhill Haven. *N Lin* 4B **38**
Grafton. *N Yor* 4D **29**
Graianrhyd. *Den* 3A **48**
Graig-fechan. *Den* 3A **48**
Grainsby. *Linc* 3C **46**
Grainthorpe. *Linc* 3D **47**
Grainthorpe Fen. *Linc* 3D **47**
Graiselound. *N Lin* 3D **45**
Granby. *Notts* 4D **53**
Grange. *Cumb* 3D **17**
Grange. *Mers* 4A **40**
Grangemill. *Derbs* 3E **51**
Grange Moor. *W Yor* 1E **43**
Grange-over-Sands. *Cumb* 3F **25**
Grange, The. *N Yor* 1E **29**
Grangetown. *Red C* 2E **21**
Grange Villa. *Dur* 3B **14**
Gransmoor. *E Yor* 1B **38**
Grantham. *Linc* 4F **53**
Grantley. *N Yor* 4B **28**
Grantshouse. *Scot* 1A **4**
Grappenhall. *Warr* 4E **41**
Grasby. *Linc* 2A **46**
Grasmere. *Cumb* 4E **17**
Grasscroft. *G Man* 2B **42**
Grassendale. *Mers* 4B **40**
Grassgarth. *Cumb* 4E **11**
Grassholme. *Dur* 2E **19**
Grassington. *N Yor* 4F **27**
Grassmoor. *Derbs* 2A **52**
Grassthorpe. *Notts* 2D **53**
Gratton. *Staf* 3B **50**
Gravel Hole. *G Man* 2B **42**
Grayingham. *Linc* 3F **45**
Grayrigg. *Cumb* 1A **26**
Grayson Green. *Cumb* 2A **16**
Graythorp. *Hart* 2E **21**
Greasby. *Mers* 4A **40**
Greaseborough. *S Yor* 3A **44**
Great Altcar. *Lanc* 2B **40**
Great Asby. *Cumb* 3B **18**
Great Ayton. *N Yor* 3E **21**
Great Barrow. *Ches* 2C **48**
Great Barugh. *N Yor* 3A **30**
Great Bavington. *Nmbd* 4B **8**
Great Blencow. *Cumb* 1F **17**
Great Broughton. *Cumb* 1B **16**
Great Broughton. *N Yor* 4E **21**
Great Budworth. *Ches* 1E **49**
Great Burdon. *Darl* 3C **20**
Great Busby. *N Yor* 4E **21**
Great Carlton. *Linc* 4E **47**
Great Chilton. *Dur* 1B **20**
Great Cliff. *W Yor* 1F **43**
Great Clifton. *Cumb* 2B **16**
Great Coates. *NE Lin* 1C **46**
Great Corby. *Cumb* 3F **11**
Great Cowden. *E Yor* 2C **38**
Great Crakehall. *N Yor* 2B **28**
Great Crosby. *Mers* 3B **40**
Great Cubley. *Derbs* 4D **51**
Great Eccleston. *Lanc* 2C **32**
Great Edstone. *N Yor* 2A **30**
Great Eppleton. *Tyne* 4C **14**
Great Fencote. *N Yor* 1B **28**
Great Gate. *Staf* 4C **50**
Great Givendale. *E Yor* 1E **37**
Great Gonerby. *Linc* 4F **53**
Great Habton. *N Yor* 3A **30**
Great Hale. *Linc* 4B **54**
Greatham. *Hart* 2D **21**
Great Harwood. *Lanc* 3F **33**
Great Hatfield. *E Yor* 2B **38**
Great Heck. *N Yor* 4B **36**
Great Horton. *W Yor* 3D **35**
Great Houghton. *S Yor* 2A **44**
Great Hucklow. *Derbs* 1D **51**
Great Kelk. *E Yor* 1B **38**
Great Kendale. *E Yor* 4D **31**
Great Langdale. *Cumb* 4D **17**
Great Langton. *N Yor* 1B **28**
Great Limber. *Linc* 2B **46**
Great Longstone. *Derbs* 1E **51**
Great Lumley. *Dur* 4B **14**
Great Marton. *Bkpl* 3B **32**
Great Mitton. *Lanc* 3F **33**
Great Musgrave. *Cumb* 3C **18**
Great Ormside. *Cumb* 3C **18**
Great Orton. *Cumb* 3E **11**
Great Ouseburn. *N Yor* 4D **29**
Great Plumpton. *Lanc* 3B **32**
Great Preston. *W Yor* 4A **36**
Great Ryle. *Nmbd* 1C **8**
Great Salkeld. *Cumb* 1A **18**
Great Sankey. *Warr* 4D **41**
Great Smeaton. *N Yor* 4C **20**
Great Stainton. *Darl* 2C **20**
Great Steeping. *Linc* 2E **55**
Great Strickland. *Cumb* 2A **18**
Great Sturton. *Linc* 1C **54**
Great Sutton. *Ches* 1B **48**
Great Swinburne. *Nmbd* 1E **13**
Great Thirkleby. *N Yor* 3D **29**
Great Tosson. *Nmbd* 2C **8**
Great Tows. *Linc* 3C **46**
Great Urswick. *Cumb* 3D **25**
Great Whittington. *Nmbd* 1F **13**
Grebby. *Linc* 2E **55**
Greencroft. *Dur* 3A **14**
Greencroft Hall. *Dur* 4A **14**
Greendykes. *Nmbd* 4C **4**
Green End. *N Yor* 4B **22**
Greenfield. *Flin* 1A **48**
Greenfield. *G Man* 2B **42**
Greengill. *Cumb* 1C **16**
Greenhalgh. *Lanc* 3C **32**
Green Hammerton. *N Yor* 1A **36**
Greenhaugh. *Nmbd* 4F **7**
Greenhead. *Nmbd* 2B **12**
Greenhill. *Dum* 1C **10**
Greenhill. *S Yor* 4F **43**
Greenhow Hill. *N Yor* 4A **28**
Greenlea. *Dum* 1B **10**
Greenmount. *G Man* 1F **41**
Greenodd. *Cumb* 2E **25**
Greenrow. *Cumb* 3C **10**
Greenside. *Tyne* 2A **14**
Greensidehill. *Nmbd* 1B **8**
Green, The. *Cumb* 2C **24**
Greenwell. *Cumb* 3A **12**
Greetham. *Linc* 1D **55**
Greetland. *W Yor* 4C **34**
Gregson Lane. *Lanc* 4D **33**
Grenoside. *S Yor* 3F **43**
Gresford. *Wrex* 3B **48**
Gressingham. *Lanc* 3A **26**
Greta Bridge. *Dur* 3F **19**
Gretna. *Dum* 2E **11**
Gretna Green. *Dum* 2E **11**
Grewelthorpe. *N Yor* 3B **28**
Greygarth. *N Yor* 3A **28**
Grey Green. *N Lin* 2D **45**
Greysouthern. *Cumb* 2B **16**
Greystoke. *Cumb* 1F **17**
Greystoke Gill. *Cumb* 2F **17**
Greystones. *S Yor* 4F **43**
Gribthorpe. *E Yor* 3D **37**
Grimeford Village. *Lanc* 1E **41**
Grimethorpe. *S Yor* 2A **44**
Grimoldby. *Linc* 4D **47**
Grimsargh. *Lanc* 3D **33**
Grimsby. *NE Lin* 1C **46**
Grimshaw. *Bkbn* 4F **33**
Grimshaw Green. *Lanc* 1C **40**
Grimston. *E Yor* 3C **38**
Grimston. *York* 1C **36**
Grindale. *E Yor* 3E **31**
Grindleford. *Derbs* 1E **51**
Grindleton. *Lanc* 2F **33**
Grindley Brook. *Shrp* 4D **49**
Grindlow. *Derbs* 1D **51**
Grindon. *Nmbd* 2B **4**
Grindon. *Staf* 3C **50**
Gringley on the Hill. *Notts* 3D **45**
Grinsdale. *Cumb* 3E **11**
Grinton. *N Yor* 1F **27**
Gristhorpe. *N Yor* 2D **31**
Grizebeck. *Cumb* 2D **25**
Grizedale. *Cumb* 1E **25**
Grosmont. *N Yor* 4B **22**
Grove. *Notts* 1D **53**
Grovehill. *E Yor* 3A **38**
Grove, The. *Dum* 1A **10**
Guide. *Bkbn* 4F **33**
Guide Post. *Nmbd* 4E **9**
Guilden Sutton. *Ches* 2C **48**
Guisborough. *Red C* 3F **21**
Guiseley. *W Yor* 2D **35**
Gunby. *E Yor* 3D **37**
Gunnerside. *N Yor* 1E **27**
Gunnerton. *Nmbd* 1E **13**
Gunness. *N Lin* 1E **45**
Gunsgreenhill. *Scot* 1B **4**
Gunthorpe. *N Lin* 3E **45**
Gunthorpe. *Notts* 4C **52**
Guyzance. *Nmbd* 2E **9**
Gwernaffield. *Flin* 2A **48**
Gwernymynydd. *Flin* 2A **48**
Gwersyllt. *Wrex* 3B **48**
Gwynfryn. *Wrex* 3A **48**
Gyfelia. *Wrex* 4B **48**

H

Habergham. *Lanc* 3A **34**
Habrough. *NE Lin* 1B **46**
Haceby. *Linc* 4A **54**
Hackenthorpe. *S Yor* 4A **44**
Hackforth. *N Yor* 1B **28**
Hackness. *N Yor* 1C **30**
Hackthorn. *Linc* 4F **45**
Hackthorpe. *Cumb* 2A **18**
Hadden. *Scot* 3A **4**
Haddington. *Linc* 2F **53**
Hadfield. *Derbs* 3C **42**
Hady. *Derbs* 1A **52**
Haggate. *Lanc* 3A **34**
Haggbeck. *Cumb* 1F **11**
Haggerston. *Nmbd* 2C **4**
Hagnaby. *Linc* 2D **55**
Hagworthingham. *Linc* 2D **55**
Haigh. *G Man* 2E **41**
Haigh Moor. *W Yor* 4E **35**
Haighton Green. *Lanc* 3D **33**
Haile. *Cumb* 4B **16**
Hainton. *Linc* 4B **46**
Hainworth. *W Yor* 3C **34**
Haisthorpe. *E Yor* 4E **31**

Halam—Holme St Cuthbert

Halam. *Notts* 3C **52**
Hale. *Cumb* 3A **26**
Hale. *G Man* 4F **41**
Hale. *Hal* 4C **40**
Hale Bank. *Hal* 4C **40**
Halebarns. *G Man* 4F **41**
Hales. *Staf* 4F **49**
Hales Green. *Derbs* 4D **51**
Halewood. *Mers* 4C **40**
Halfpenny. *Cumb* 2A **26**
Halfway. *S Yor* 4A **44**
Halifax. *W Yor* 4C **34**
Halkyn. *Flin* 1A **48**
Hallam Fields. *Derbs* 4A **52**
Hallands, The. *N Lin* 4A **38**
Hallbank. *Cumb* 1B **26**
Hallbankgate. *Cumb* 3A **12**
Hall Dunnerdale. *Cumb* 1D **25**
Hallgarth. *Dur* 4C **14**
Hall Green. *Ches* 3A **50**
Hall Green. *W Yor* 1F **43**
Hall Green. *Wrex* 4C **48**
Hallington. *Linc* 4D **47**
Hallington. *Nmbd* 1E **13**
Halloughton. *Notts* 3C **52**
Hallowsgate. *Ches* 2D **49**
Hallthwaites. *Cumb* 2C **24**
Hall Waberthwaite. *Cumb* 1C **24**
Halmer End. *Staf* 4A **50**
Halsall. *Lanc* 1B **40**
Halsham. *E Yor* 4C **38**
Haltcliff Bridge. *Cumb* 1E **17**
Haltham. *Linc* 2C **54**
Haltoft End. *Linc* 4D **55**
Halton. *Hal* 4D **41**
Halton. *Lanc* 4A **26**
Halton. *Nmbd* 2E **13**
Halton. *W Yor* 3F **35**
Halton. *Wrex* 4B **48**
Halton East. *N Yor* 1C **34**
Halton Fenside. *Linc* 2E **55**
Halton Gill. *N Yor* 3D **27**
Halton Holegate. *Linc* 2E **55**
Halton Lea Gate. *Nmbd* 3B **12**
Halton Moor. *W Yor* 3F **35**
Halton Shields. *Nmbd* 2F **13**
Halton West. *N Yor* 1A **34**
Haltwhistle. *Nmbd* 2C **12**
Hambleton. *Lanc* 2B **32**
Hambleton. *N Yor* 3B **36**
Hameringham. *Linc* 2D **55**
Hampole. *S Yor* 1B **44**
Hampsthwaite. *N Yor* 1E **35**
Hampton Heath. *Ches* 4D **49**
Hamsterley. *Dur* 3A **14** (nr. Consett)
Hamsterley. *Dur* 1A **20** (nr. Wolsingham)
Hamsterley Mill. *Dur* 3A **14**
Hanchurch. *Staf* 4A **50**
Handbridge. *Ches* 2C **48**
Handforth. *Ches* 4A **42**
Handley. *Ches* 3C **48**
Handley. *Derbs* 2F **51**
Handsworth. *S Yor* 4A **44**
Hanford. *Stoke* 4A **50**
Hankelow. *Ches* 4E **49**
Hanley. *Stoke* 4A **50**
Hanlith. *N Yor* 4E **27**
Hanmer. *Wrex* 4C **48**
Hannah. *Linc* 1F **55**
Hapsford. *Ches* 1C **48**
Hapton. *Lanc* 3F **33**
Harbottle. *Nmbd* 2B **8**
Harby. *Notts* 1E **53**
Harden. *W Yor* 3C **34**
Hardings Wood. *Ches* 3A **50**
Hardraw. *N Yor* 1D **27**
Hardstoft. *Derbs* 2A **52**
Hardwick. *S Yor* 4A **44**
Hardwick. *Stoc T* 2D **21**
Hardwick Village. *Notts* 1C **52**
Hareby. *Linc* 2D **55**
Hareden. *Lanc* 1E **33**
Harehill. *Derbs* 4D **51**
Harehills. *W Yor* 3F **35**
Harehope. *Nmbd* 4C **4**
Harelaw. *Dum* 1F **11**
Harelaw. *Dur* 3A **14**
Harescеugh. *Cumb* 4B **12**
Haresfinch. *Mers* 3D **41**
Harewood. *W Yor* 2F **35**
Hargatewall. *Derbs* 1D **51**
Hargrave. *Ches* 2C **48**
Harker. *Cumb* 2E **11**
Harlequin. *Notts* 4C **52**
Harley. *S Yor* 3F **43**
Harlington. *S Yor* 2A **44**
Harlow Hill. *Nmbd* 2F **13**
Harlsey Castle. *N Yor* 1D **29**
Harlthorpe. *E Yor* 3D **37**
Harmby. *N Yor* 2A **28**
Harmston. *Linc* 2F **53**
Harnham. *Nmbd* 4C **8**
Harome. *N Yor* 2F **29**
Harpham. *E Yor* 4D **31**
Harpswell. *Linc* 4F **45**
Harpurhey. *G Man* 2A **42**
Harpur Hill. *Derbs* 1C **50**
Harraby. *Cumb* 3F **11**
Harrington. *Cumb* 2A **16**
Harrington. *Linc* 1D **55**
Harriseahead. *Staf* 3A **50**
Harriston. *Cumb* 4C **10**
Harrogate. *N Yor* 1F **35**
Harrop Dale. *G Man* 2C **42**
Harrowgate Hill. *Darl* 3B **20**
Harswell. *E Yor* 2E **37**
Hart. *Hart* 1D **21**
Hartburn. *Nmbd* 4C **8**
Hartburn. *Stoc T* 3D **21**
Hartford. *Ches* 1E **49**
Harthill. *Ches* 3D **49**
Harthill. *S Yor* 4A **44**
Hartington. *Derbs* 2D **51**
Hartlepool. *Hart* 1E **21**
Hartley. *Cumb* 4C **18**
Hartley. *Nmbd* 1C **14**
Hartoft End. *N Yor* 1A **30**
Harton. *N Yor* 4A **30**
Harton. *Tyne* 2C **14**
Hartshead. *W Yor* 4D **35**
Hartsop. *Cumb* 3F **17**
Hart Station. *Hart* 1D **21**
Hartwood. *Lanc* 1D **41**
Harwood. *Dur* 1D **19**
Harwood. *G Man* 1F **41**
Harwood Dale. *N Yor* 1C **30**
Harworth. *Notts* 3C **44**
Haskayne. *Lanc* 2B **40**
Hasland. *Derbs* 2F **51**
Haslingden. *Lanc* 4F **33**
Haslingden Grane. *Lanc* 4F **33**
Haslington. *Ches* 3F **49**
Hassall. *Ches* 3F **49**
Hassall Green. *Ches* 3F **49**
Hassendean. *Scot* 1D **7**
Hassness. *Cumb* 3C **16**
Hassop. *Derbs* 1E **51**
Hasthorpe. *Linc* 2E **55**
Haswell. *Dur* 4C **14**
Haswell Plough. *Dur* 4C **14**
Hatchmere. *Ches* 1D **49**
Hatcliffe. *NE Lin* 2C **46**
Hatfield. *S Yor* 2C **44**
Hatfield Woodhouse. *S Yor* 2C **44**
Hathersage. *Derbs* 4E **43**
Hathersage Booths. *Derbs* 4E **43**
Hatherton. *Ches* 4E **49**
Hattersley. *G Man* 3B **42**
Hatton. *Linc* 1B **54**
Hatton. *Warr* 4D **41**
Hatton Heath. *Ches* 2C **48**
Haugh. *Linc* 1E **55**
Haugham. *Linc* 4D **47**
Haugh Head. *Nmbd* 4C **4**
Haughton. *Notts* 1C **52**
Haughton Green. *G Man* 3B **42**
Haughton le Skerne. *Darl* 3C **20**
Haughton Moss. *Ches* 3D **49**
Hauxley. *Nmbd* 2E **9**
Havannah. *Ches* 2A **50**
Haven Bank. *Linc* 3C **54**
Havenside. *E Yor* 4B **38**
Havercroft. *W Yor* 1F **43**
Haverigg. *Cumb* 3C **24**
Haverthwaite. *Cumb* 2E **25**
Haverton Hill. *Stoc T* 2D **21**
Hawarden. *Flin* 2B **48**
Hawcoat. *Cumb* 3D **25**
Hawes. *N Yor* 2D **27**
Hawick. *Scot* 1D **7**
Hawk Green. *G Man* 4B **42**
Hawkhill. *Nmbd* 1E **9**
Hawksdale. *Cumb* 4E **11**
Hawkshaw. *G Man* 1F **41**
Hawkshead. *Cumb* 1E **25**
Hawkshead Hill. *Cumb* 1E **25**
Hawkswick. *N Yor* 3E **27**
Hawksworth. *Notts* 4D **53**
Hawksworth. *W Yor* 2D **35**
Hawnby. *N Yor* 2E **29**
Haworth. *W Yor* 3C **34**
Hawthorn. *Dur* 4D **15**
Hawthorn Hill. *Linc* 3C **54**
Hawton. *Notts* 3D **53**
Haxby. *York* 1C **36**
Haxey. *N Lin* 3D **45**
Haydock. *Mers* 3D **41**
Haydon Bridge. *Nmbd* 2D **13**
Hayfield. *Derbs* 4C **42**
Hayton. *Cumb* 4C **10** (nr. Aspatria)
Hayton. *Cumb* 3A **12** (nr. Brampton)
Hayton. *E Yor* 2E **37**
Hayton. *Notts* 4D **45**
Hazel Grove. *G Man* 4B **42**
Hazelhead. *S Yor* 2D **43**
Hazelwood. *Derbs* 4F **51**
Hazlerigg. *Tyne* 1B **14**
Hazles. *Staf* 4C **50**
Hazon. *Nmbd* 2D **9**
Headingley. *W Yor* 3E **35**
Headlam. *Dur* 3A **20**
Headon. *Notts* 1D **53**
Heads Nook. *Cumb* 3F **11**
Heage. *Derbs* 3F **51**
Healaugh. *N Yor* 1F **27** (nr. Grinton)
Healaugh. *N Yor* 2B **36** (nr. York)
Heald Green. *G Man* 4A **42**
Healey. *G Man* 1A **42**
Healey. *Nmbd* 3F **13**
Healey. *N Yor* 2A **28**
Healeyfield. *Dur* 4F **13**
Healey Hall. *Nmbd* 3F **13**
Healing. *NE Lin* 1C **46**
Heanor. *Derbs* 4A **52**
Heapham. *Linc* 4E **45**
Heath. *Derbs* 2A **52**
Heathcote. *Derbs* 2D **51**
Heathfield. *Cumb* 4C **10**
Heathhall. *Dum* 1A **10**
Heath, The. *Staf* 4C **50**
Heatley. *G Man* 4F **41**
Heaton. *Lanc* 4F **25**
Heaton. *Staf* 2B **50**
Heaton. *Tyne* 2B **14**
Heaton. *W Yor* 3D **35**
Heaton Moor. *G Man* 3A **42**
Heaton's Bridge. *Lanc* 1C **40**
Hebburn. *Tyne* 2C **14**
Hebden. *N Yor* 4F **27**
Hebden Bridge. *W Yor* 4B **34**
Hebden Green. *Ches* 2E **49**
Hebron. *Nmbd* 4D **9**
Heck. *Dum* 1B **10**
Heckdyke. *Notts* 3D **45**
Heckington. *Linc* 4B **54**
Heckmondwike. *W Yor* 4E **35**
Heddon-on-the-Wall. *Nmbd* 2A **14**
Hedley on the Hill. *Nmbd* 3F **13**
Hedon. *E Yor* 4B **38**
Heighington. *Darl* 2B **20**
Heighington. *Linc* 2A **54**
Hellifield. *N Yor* 1A **34**
Helmington Row. *Dur* 1A **20**
Helmshore. *Lanc* 4F **33**
Helmsley. *N Yor* 2F **29**
Helperby. *N Yor* 4D **29**
Helperthorpe. *N Yor* 3C **30**
Helpringham. *Linc* 4B **54**
Helsby. *Ches* 1C **48**
Helsey. *Linc* 1F **55**
Helton. *Cumb* 2A **18**
Helwith. *N Yor* 4F **19**
Helwith Bridge. *N Yor* 4D **27**
Helygain. *Flin* 1A **48**
Hemingbrough. *N Yor* 3C **36**
Hemingby. *Linc* 1C **54**
Hemingfield. *S Yor* 2F **43**
Hemlington. *Midd* 3D **21**
Hempholme. *E Yor* 1A **38**
Hemswell. *Linc* 3F **45**
Hemswell Cliff. *Linc* 4F **45**
Hemsworth. *W Yor* 1A **44**
Henbury. *Ches* 1A **50**
Hendon. *Tyne* 3D **15**
Hensall. *N Yor* 4B **36**
Henshaw. *Nmbd* 2C **12**
Hensingham. *Cumb* 3A **16**
Hepburn. *Nmbd* 4C **4**
Hepple. *Nmbd* 2B **8**
Hepscott. *Nmbd* 4E **9**
Heptonstall. *W Yor* 4B **34**
Hepworth. *W Yor* 2D **43**
Hermitage. *Scot* 3D **7**
Herrington. *Tyne* 3C **14**
Hesketh. *Lanc* 4C **32**
Hesketh Bank. *Lanc* 4C **32**
Hesketh Lane. *Lanc* 2E **33**
Hesket Newmarket. *Cumb* 1E **17**
Heskin Green. *Lanc* 1D **41**
Hesleden. *Dur* 1D **21**
Hesleyside. *Nmbd* 4A **8**
Heslington. *York* 1C **36**
Hessay. *York* 1B **36**
Hessle. *E Yor* 4A **38**
Hest Bank. *Lanc* 4F **25**
Heswall. *Mers* 4A **40**
Hethersgill. *Cumb* 2F **11**
Hetherside. *Cumb* 2F **11**
Hethpool. *Nmbd* 4A **4**
Hett. *Dur* 1B **20**
Hetton. *N Yor* 1B **34**
Hetton-le-Hole. *Tyne* 4C **14**
Hetton Steads. *Nmbd* 3C **4**
Heugh. *Nmbd* 1F **13**
Heversham. *Cumb* 2F **25**
Heworth. *York* 1C **36**
Hexham. *Nmbd* 2E **13**
Heydour. *Linc* 4A **54**
Heysham. *Lanc* 4F **25**
Heywood. *G Man* 1A **42**
Hibaldstow. *N Lin* 2F **45**
Hickleton. *S Yor* 2A **44**
High Ackworth. *W Yor* 1A **44**
Higham. *Derbs* 3F **51**
Higham. *Lanc* 3A **34**
Higham. *S Yor* 2F **43**
Higham Dykes. *Nmbd* 1A **14**
High Angerton. *Nmbd* 4C **8**
High Bankhill. *Cumb* 4A **12**
High Bentham. *N Yor* 4B **26**
High Biggins. *Cumb* 3B **26**
High Birkwith. *N Yor* 3C **26**
High Borrans. *Cumb* 4F **17**
High Bradfield. *S Yor* 3E **43**
Highbridge. *Cumb* 4E **11**
Highburton. *W Yor* 1D **43**
High Buston. *Nmbd* 2E **9**
High Callerton. *Nmbd* 1A **14**
High Carlingill. *Cumb* 4B **18**
High Catton. *E Yor* 1D **37**
High Church. *Nmbd* 4D **9**
High Coniscliffe. *Darl* 3B **20**
High Crosby. *Cumb* 3F **11**
High Eggborough. *N Yor* 4B **36**
High Ellington. *N Yor* 2A **28**
Higher Ballam. *Lanc* 3B **32**
Higher Bartle. *Lanc* 3D **33**
Higher Dinting. *Derbs* 3C **42**
Higher End. *G Man* 2D **41**
Higher Heysham. *Lanc* 4F **25**
Higher Hurdsfield. *Ches* 1B **50**
Higher Kinnerton. *Flin* 2B **48**
Higher Penwortham. *Lanc* 4D **33**
Higher Poynton. *Ches* 4B **42**
Higher Shotton. *Flin* 2B **48**
Higher Shurlach. *Ches* 1E **49**
Higher Walton. *Lanc* 4D **33**
Higher Walton. *Warr* 4E **41**
Higher Wheelton. *Lanc* 4E **33**
Higher Whitley. *Ches* 1E **49**
Higher Wincham. *Ches* 1E **49**
Higher Wych. *Ches* 4C **48**
High Etherley. *Dur* 2A **20**
High Ferry. *Linc* 4D **55**
Highfield. *E Yor* 3D **37**
Highfield. *Tyne* 3A **14**
Highfields. *Nmbd* 1B **4**
High Grange. *Dur* 1A **20**
High Green. *Cumb* 4F **17**
High Green. *S Yor* 3F **43**
High Green. *W Yor* 1D **43**
Highgreen Manor. *Nmbd* 3A **8**
High Harrington. *Cumb* 2B **16**
High Haswell. *Dur* 4C **14**
High Hawkser. *N Yor* 4C **22**
High Hesket. *Cumb* 4F **11**
High Hesleden. *Dur* 1D **21**
High Hoyland. *S Yor* 2E **43**
High Hunsley. *E Yor* 3F **37**
High Hutton. *N Yor* 4A **30**
High Ireby. *Cumb* 1D **17**
High Kilburn. *N Yor* 3E **29**
High Killerby. *N Yor* 2D **31**
High Knipe. *Cumb* 3A **18**
High Lands. *Dur* 2A **20**
Highlane. *Ches* 2A **50**
Highlane. *Derbs* 4A **44**
High Lane. *G Man* 4B **42**
Highlaws. *Cumb* 4C **10**
High Legh. *Ches* 4E **41**
High Leven. *Stoc T* 3D **21**
High Longthwaite. *Cumb* 4D **11**
High Lorton. *Cumb* 2C **16**
High Marishes. *N Yor* 3B **30**
High Marnham. *Notts* 1E **53**
High Melton. *S Yor* 2B **44**
High Mickley. *Nmbd* 2F **13**
Highmoor. *Cumb* 4D **11**
High Moor. *Lanc* 1D **41**
High Mowthorpe. *N Yor* 4B **30**
High Newport. *Tyne* 3C **14**
High Newton. *Cumb* 2F **25**
High Newton-by-the-Sea. *Nmbd* 4E **5**
High Nibthwaite. *Cumb* 2D **25**
High Park. *Mers* 1B **40**
High Row. *Cumb* 1E **17**
High Scales. *Cumb* 4C **10**
High Shaw. *N Yor* 1D **27**
High Side. *Cumb* 1D **17**
High Spen. *Tyne* 2A **14**
High Stoop. *Dur* 4A **14**
Hightae. *Dum* 1B **10**
High Throston. *Hart* 1D **21**
Hightown. *Ches* 2A **50**
Hightown. *Mers* 2A **40**
High Toynton. *Linc* 2C **54**
High Trewhitt. *Nmbd* 2C **8**
High Westwood. *Dur* 3A **14**
High Worsall. *N Yor* 4C **20**
High Wray. *Cumb* 1E **25**
Hilderstone. *Staf* 4B **50**
Hilderthorpe. *E Yor* 4E **31**
Hillam. *N Yor* 4B **36**
Hillbeck. *Cumb* 3C **18**
Hillcliffiane. *Derbs* 4E **51**
Hilldyke. *Linc* 4D **55**
Hill End. *Dur* 1F **19**
Hill End. *N Yor* 1C **34**
Hillsborough. *S Yor* 3F **43**
Hillside. *Mers* 1B **40**
Hill Side. *W Yor* 1D **43**
Hill Somersal. *Derbs* 4D **51**
Hillstown. *Derbs* 2A **52**
Hill, The. *Cumb* 2C **24**
Hill Top. *Dur* 2E **19** (nr. Barnard Castle)
Hill Top. *Dur* 4B **14** (nr. Durham)
Hill Top. *Dur* 3A **14** (nr. Stanley)
Hilston. *E Yor* 3C **38**
Hilton. *Cumb* 2C **18**
Hilton. *Dur* 2A **20**
Hilton. *Stoc T* 3D **21**
Hincaster. *Cumb* 2A **26**
Hinchcliffe Mill. *W Yor* 2D **43**
Hinderwell. *N Yor* 3A **22**
Hindley. *G Man* 2E **41**
Hindley. *Nmbd* 3F **13**
Hindley Green. *G Man* 2E **41**
Hipperholme. *W Yor* 4D **35**
Hipsburn. *Nmbd* 1E **9**
Hipswell. *N Yor* 1A **28**
Hirst. *Nmbd* 4E **9**
Hirst Courtney. *N Yor* 4C **36**
Hirwaen. *Den* 2A **48**
Hive. *E Yor* 3E **37**
Hobkirk. *Scot* 1D **7**
Hobson. *Dur* 3A **14**
Hockerton. *Notts* 3D **53**
Hoddlesden. *Bkbn* 4F **33**
Hoddomcross. *Dum* 1C **10**
Hodthorpe. *Derbs* 1B **52**
Hoff. *Cumb* 3B **18**
Hoffleet Stow. *Linc* 4C **54**
Hoghton. *Lanc* 4E **33**
Hoghton Bottoms. *Lanc* 4E **33**
Hognaston. *Derbs* 3E **51**
Hogsthorpe. *Linc* 1F **55**
Holbeck. *Notts* 1B **52**
Holbeck. *W Yor* 3E **35**
Holbrook. *Derbs* 4F **51**
Holbrook. *S Yor* 4A **44**
Holburn. *Nmbd* 3C **4**
Holcombe. *G Man* 1F **41**
Holcombe Brook. *G Man* 1F **41**
Holden. *Lanc* 2F **33**
Holdingham. *Linc* 4A **54**
Holker. *Cumb* 3E **25**
Holland Fen. *Linc* 4C **54**
Holland Lees. *Lanc* 2D **41**
Hollinfare. *Warr* 3E **41**
Hollington. *Derbs* 4E **51**
Hollington. *Staf* 4C **50**
Hollington Grove. *Derbs* 4E **51**
Hollingworth. *G Man* 3C **42**
Hollins. *Derbs* 1F **51**
Hollins. *G Man* 2A **42** (nr. Bury)
Hollins. *G Man* 2A **42** (nr. Middleton)
Hollinsclough. *Staf* 2C **50**
Hollinthorpe. *W Yor* 3F **35**
Hollinwood. *G Man* 2B **42**
Hollinwood. *Shrp* 4D **49**
Holloway. *Derbs* 3F **51**
Hollow Meadows. *S Yor* 4E **43**
Hollows. *Dum* 1E **11**
Holly Hill. *N Yor* 4A **20**
Hollyhurst. *Ches* 4D **49**
Hollym. *E Yor* 4D **39**
Hollywood. *Staf* 4B **50**
Holmbridge. *W Yor* 2D **43**
Holme. *Cumb* 3A **26**
Holme. *N Lin* 2F **45**
Holme. *N Yor* 2C **28**
Holme. *Notts* 3E **53**
Holme. *W Yor* 2D **43**
Holme Chapel. *Lanc* 4A **34**
Holme Lane. *Notts* 4C **52**
Holme-on-Spalding-Moor. *E Yor* 3E **37**
Holme on the Wolds. *E Yor* 2F **37**
Holme Pierrepont. *Notts* 4C **52**
Holmes. *Lanc* 1C **40**
Holme St Cuthbert. *Cumb* 4C **10**

Knypersley—Makeney

Knypersley. *Staf* 3A **50**
Krumlin. *W Yor* 1C **42**

L

Laceby. *NE Lin* 2C **46**
Lach Dennis. *Ches* 1F **49**
Lache. *Ches* 2B **48**
Lade Bank. *Linc* 3D **55**
Lady Green. *Mers* 2B **40**
Lady Hall. *Cumb* 2C **24**
Ladykirk. *Scot* 2A **4**
Laithes. *Cumb* 1F **17**
Laithkirk. *Dur* 2E **19**
Lakeside. *Cumb* 2E **25**
Lambden. *Scot* 2A **4**
Lamberhead Green. *G Man* 2D **41**
Lamberton. *Scot* 1B **4**
Lambley. *Nmbd* 3B **12**
Lambley. *Notts* 4C **52**
Lamesley. *Tyne* 3B **14**
Lamonby. *Cumb* 1F **17**
Lamplugh. *Cumb* 2B **16**
Lancaster. *Lanc* 4F **25**
Lanchester. *Dur* 4A **14**
Land Gate. *G Man* 2D **41**
Lane Bottom. *Lanc* 3A **34**
Lane End. *Cumb* 1C **24**
Lane Ends. *Derbs* 4E **51**
Lane Ends. *Dur* 1A **20**
Lane Ends. *Lanc* 1F **33**
Laneham. *Notts* 1E **53**
Lanehead. *Dur* 4D **13** (nr. Cowshill)
Lane Head. *Dur* 3A **20** (nr. Hutton Magna)
Lane Head. *Dur* 2F **19** (nr. Woodland)
Lane Head. *G Man* 3E **41**
Lanehead. *Nmbd* 4F **7**
Lane Head. *W Yor* 2D **43**
Lane Heads. *Lanc* 3C **32**
Lanercost. *Cumb* 2A **12**
Laneshaw Bridge. *Lanc* 2B **34**
Langar. *Notts* 4D **53**
Langbar. *N Yor* 1C **34**
Langburnshiels. *Scot* 2D **7**
Langcliffe. *N Yor* 4D **27**
Langdale End. *N Yor* 1C **30**
Langdon Beck. *Dur* 1D **19**
Langford. *Notts* 3E **53**
Langho. *Lanc* 3F **33**
Langholm. *Dum* 4B **6**
Langleeford. *Nmbd* 4B **4**
Langley. *Ches* 1B **50**
Langley. *Derbs* 4A **52**
Langley. *Nmbd* 2D **13**
Langley Common. *Derbs* 4E **51**
Langley Green. *Derbs* 4E **51**
Langley Moor. *Dur* 4B **14**
Langley Park. *Dur* 4B **14**
Langold. *Notts* 4B **44**
Langrick. *Linc* 4C **54**
Langrigg. *Cumb* 4C **10**
Langsett. *S Yor* 2E **43**
Langthorne. *N Yor* 1B **28**
Langthorpe. *N Yor* 4C **28**
Langthwaite. *N Yor* 4F **19**
Langtoft. *E Yor* 4D **31**
Langton. *Dur* 3A **20**
Langton. *Linc* 2C **54** (nr. Horncastle)
Langton. *Linc* 1D **55** (nr. Spilsby)
Langton. *N Yor* 4A **30**
Langton by Wragby. *Linc* 1B **54**
Langwathby. *Cumb* 1A **18**
Langwith. *Derbs* 1B **52**
Langworth. *Linc* 1A **54**
Lanton. *Nmbd* 3B **4**
Lanton. *Scot* 1E **7**
Larden Green. *Ches* 3D **49**
Lartington. *Dur* 3F **19**
Lastingham. *N Yor* 1A **30**
Latham. *Lanc* 2C **40**
Lathom. *Lanc* 2C **40**
Laughterton. *Linc* 1E **53**
Laughton. *Linc* 3E **45**
Laughton Common. *S Yor* 4B **44**
Laughton en le Morthen. *S Yor* 4B **44**
Laverhay. *Dum* 3A **6**
Laversdale. *Cumb* 2F **11**
Laverton. *N Yor* 3B **28**
Lavister. *Wrex* 3B **48**
Lawkland. *N Yor* 4C **26**
Laxton. *E Yor* 4D **37**
Laxton. *Notts* 2D **53**
Laycock. *W Yor* 2C **34**
Laytham. *E Yor* 3D **37**
Lazenby. *Red C* 3E **21**
Lazonby. *Cumb* 1A **18**
Lea. *Derbs* 3F **51**
Lea. *Linc* 4E **45**
Leabrooks. *Derbs* 3A **52**
Leadenham. *Linc* 3F **53**
Leadgate. *Cumb* 4C **12**
Leadgate. *Dur* 3A **14**
Leadgate. *Nmbd* 3A **14**
Leake. *N Yor* 1D **29**
Leake Common Side. *Linc* 3D **55**
Leake Fold Hill. *Linc* 3E **55**
Leake Hurn's End. *Linc* 4E **55**
Lealholm. *N Yor* 4A **22**
Leam. *Derbs* 1E **51**
Leamside. *Dur* 4C **14**
Lease Rigg. *N Yor* 4B **22**
Leasgill. *Cumb* 2F **25**
Leasingham. *Linc* 4A **54**
Leasingthorne. *Dur* 2B **20**
Leasowe. *Mers* 3A **40**
Leathley. *N Yor* 2E **35**
Lea Town. *Lanc* 3C **32**
Leavening. *N Yor* 4A **30**
Lea Yeat. *Cumb* 2C **26**
Leazes. *Dur* 3A **14**
Lebberston. *N Yor* 2D **31**
Leck. *Lanc* 3B **26**
Leconfield. *E Yor* 2A **38**
Ledsham. *Ches* 1B **48**
Ledsham. *W Yor* 4A **36**
Ledston. *W Yor* 4A **36**
Lee. *Lanc* 1D **33**
Leece. *Cumb* 4D **25**
Leeds. *W Yor* 3E **35**
Leeds & Bradford Airport. *W Yor* 2E **35**
Lee Head. *Derbs* 3C **42**
Leek. *Staf* 3B **50**
Leekbrook. *Staf* 3B **50**
Leeming. *N Yor* 2B **28**
Leeming Bar. *N Yor* 1B **28**
Lee Moor. *W Yor* 4F **35**
Lees. *Derbs* 4E **51**
Lees. *G Man* 2B **42**
Lees. *W Yor* 3C **34**
Leeswood. *Flin* 3A **48**
Leftwich. *Ches* 1E **49**
Legbourne. *Linc* 4D **47**
Legburthwaite. *Cumb* 3E **17**
Legsby. *Linc* 4B **46**
Leigh. *G Man* 2E **41**
Leighton. *N Yor* 3A **28**
Leitholm. *Scot* 2A **4**
Lelley. *E Yor* 3C **38**
Lemington. *Tyne* 2A **14**
Lemmington Hall. *Nmbd* 1D **9**
Lempitlaw. *Scot* 3A **4**
Lenacre. *Cumb* 2B **26**
Lennel. *Scot* 2A **4**
Lenton. *Nott* 4B **52**
Leppington. *N Yor* 4A **30**
Lepton. *W Yor* 1E **43**
Lesbury. *Nmbd* 1E **9**
Lessonhall. *Cumb* 3D **11**
Letwell. *S Yor* 4B **44**
Leven. *E Yor* 2B **38**
Levens. *Cumb* 2F **25**
Levenshulme. *G Man* 3A **42**
Leverton. *Linc* 4E **55**
Leverton Lucasgate. *Linc* 4E **55**
Leverton Outgate. *Linc* 4E **55**
Levisham. *N Yor* 1B **30**
Leyburn. *N Yor* 1A **28**
Leycett. *Staf* 4F **49**
Leyland. *Lanc* 4D **33**
Leymoor. *W Yor* 1D **43**
Lidgett. *Notts* 2C **52**
Light Oaks. *Stoke* 4B **50**
Lightwood. *Staf* 4C **50**
Lightwood. *Stoke* 4B **50**
Lightwood Green. *Ches* 4E **49**
Lightwood Green. *Wrex* 4B **48**
Lilburn Tower. *Nmbd* 4C **4**
Lilliesleaf. *Scot* 1D **7**
Limbrick. *Lanc* 1E **41**
Lime Kiln Nook. *Cumb* 4E **11**
Limestone Brae. *Nmbd* 4C **12**
Linby. *Notts* 3B **52**
Lincluden. *Dum* 1A **10**
Lincoln. *Linc* 1F **53**
Lindale. *Cumb* 2F **25**
Lindal in Furness. *Cumb* 3D **25**
Lingdale. *Red C* 3F **21**
Lingyclose Head. *Cumb* 3E **11**
Linshiels. *Nmbd* 2A **8**
Linstock. *Cumb* 3F **11**
Linthwaite. *W Yor* 1D **43**
Lintlaw. *Scot* 1A **4**
Linton. *N Yor* 4E **27**
Linton. *Scot* 4A **4**
Linton. *W Yor* 2F **35**
Linton Colliery. *Nmbd* 3E **9**
Linton-on-Ouse. *N Yor* 4D **29**
Lintzford. *Tyne* 3A **14**
Lintzgarth. *Dur* 4E **13**
Linwood. *Linc* 4B **46**
Liscard. *Mers* 3B **40**
Lissett. *E Yor* 1B **38**
Lissington. *Linc* 4B **46**
Litherland. *Mers* 3B **40**
Littemill. *Nmbd* 1E **9**
Little Airmyn. *N Yor* 4D **37**
Little Asby. *Cumb* 4B **18**
Little Ayton. *N Yor* 3E **21**
Little Bampton. *Cumb* 3D **11**
Little Barrow. *Ches* 2C **48**
Little Barugh. *N Yor* 3A **30**
Little Bavington. *Nmbd* 1E **13**
Little Bispham. *Bkpl* 2B **32**
Little Blencow. *Cumb* 1F **17**
Little Bollington. *Ches* 4F **41**
Littleborough. *G Man* 1B **42**
Littleborough. *Notts* 4E **45**
Little Broughton. *Cumb* 1B **16**
Little Budworth. *Ches* 2D **49**
Little Burton. *E Yor* 2B **38**
Little Carlton. *Linc* 4D **47**
Little Carlton. *Notts* 3D **53**
Little Catwick. *E Yor* 2B **38**
Little Cawthorpe. *Linc* 4D **47**
Little Clifton. *Cumb* 2B **16**
Little Coates. *NE Lin* 2C **46**
Little Crakehall. *N Yor* 1B **28**
Little Crosby. *Mers* 2B **40**
Little Crosthwaite. *Cumb* 2D **17**
Little Cubley. *Derbs* 4D **51**
Little Driffield. *E Yor* 1A **38**
Little Eaton. *Derbs* 4F **51**
Little Eccleston. *Lanc* 2C **32**
Little Fencote. *N Yor* 1B **28**
Little Fenton. *N Yor* 3B **36**
Little Green. *Wrex* 4C **48**
Little Grimsby. *Linc* 3D **47**
Little Habton. *N Yor* 3A **30**
Little Hale. *Linc* 4B **54**
Little Hatfield. *E Yor* 2B **38**
Little Hayfield. *Derbs* 4C **42**
Little Heck. *N Yor* 4B **36**
Little Horton. *W Yor* 3D **35**
Littlehoughton. *Nmbd* 1E **9**
Little Houghton. *S Yor* 2A **44**
Little Hucklow. *Derbs* 1D **51**
Little Hulton. *G Man* 2F **41**
Little Kelk. *E Yor* 4D **31**
Little Langdale. *Cumb* 4E **17**
Little Leigh. *Ches* 1E **49**
Little Leven. *E Yor* 2A **38**
Little Lever. *G Man* 2F **41**
Little Longstone. *Derbs* 1D **51**
Littlemoor. *Derbs* 2F **51**
Little Mountain. *Flin* 2A **48**
Little Musgrave. *Cumb* 3C **18**
Little Neston. *Ches* 1B **48**
Little Newsham. *Dur* 3A **20**
Little Ormside. *Cumb* 3C **18**
Little Orton. *Cumb* 3E **11**
Little Ouseburn. *N Yor* 4D **29**
Littleover. *Derb* 4F **51**
Little Plumpton. *Lanc* 3B **32**
Little Ribston. *N Yor* 1F **35**
Little Ryle. *Nmbd* 1C **8**
Little Salkeld. *Cumb* 1A **18**
Little Singleton. *Lanc* 3B **32**
Little Smeaton. *N Yor* 1B **44**
Little Stainforth. *N Yor* 4D **27**
Little Stainton. *Darl* 2C **20**
Little Stanney. *Ches* 1C **48**
Little Steeping. *Linc* 2E **55**
Little Strickland. *Cumb* 3A **18**
Little Sutton. *Ches* 1B **48**
Little Swinburne. *Nmbd* 1E **13**
Little Thirkleby. *N Yor* 3D **29**
Little Thornton. *Lanc* 2B **32**
Littlethorpe. *N Yor* 4C **28**
Little Thorpe. *W Yor* 4D **35**
Littleton. *Ches* 2C **48**
Little Town. *Cumb* 3D **17**
Littletown. *Dur* 4C **14**
Little Town. *Lanc* 3E **33**
Little Urswick. *Cumb* 3D **25**
Little Weighton. *E Yor* 3F **37**
Litton. *Derbs* 1D **51**
Litton. *N Yor* 3E **27**
Liverpool. *Mers* 3B **40**
Liverpool Airport. *Mers* 4C **40**
Liversedge. *W Yor* 4D **35**
Liverton. *Red C* 3A **22**
Liverton Mines. *Red C* 3A **22**
Lixwm. *Flin* 1A **48**
Llanarmon-yn-Ial. *Den* 3A **48**
Llanbedr-Dyffryn-Clwyd. *Den* 3A **48**
Llandegla. *Den* 3A **48**
Llandyrnan. *Den* 4A **48**
Llanfair Dyffryn Clwyd. *Den* 3A **48**
Llanferres. *Den* 2A **48**
Llanfynydd. *Flin* 3A **48**
Llangollen. *Den* 4A **48**
Llan-y-pwll. *Wrex* 3B **48**
Llay. *Wrex* 3B **48**
Llechrydau. *Wrex* 4A **48**
Lloc. *Flin* 1A **48**
Llong. *Flin* 2A **48**
Llwynmawr. *Wrex* 4A **48**
Loanend. *Nmbd* 1B **4**
Loaningfoot. *Dum* 3A **10**
Loansdean. *Nmbd* 4E **9**
Locharbriggs. *Dum* 1A **10**
Lochfoot. *Dum* 1A **10**
Lochmaben. *Dum* 1B **10**
Lockerbie. *Dum* 1C **10**
Lockhills. *Cumb* 4A **12**
Lockington. *E Yor* 2F **37**
Lockton. *N Yor* 2B **30**
Lofthouse. *N Yor* 3A **28**
Lofthouse. *W Yor* 4F **35**
Lofthouse Gate. *W Yor* 4F **35**
Loftus. *Red C* 3A **22**
Loggerheads. *Staf* 4F **49**
Londesborough. *E Yor* 2E **37**
Londonderry. *N Yor* 2C **28**
Londonthorpe. *Linc* 4F **53**
Long Bennington. *Linc* 4E **53**
Longbenton. *Tyne* 2B **14**
Longburgh. *Cumb* 3E **11**
Longcliffe. *Derbs* 3E **51**
Longcroft. *Cumb* 3D **11**
Longdale. *Cumb* 4B **18**
Longdales. *Cumb* 4A **12**
Long Drax. *N Yor* 4C **36**
Long Duckmanton. *Derbs* 1A **52**
Long Eaton. *Derbs* 4A **52**
Longford. *Derbs* 4E **51**
Longford. *Shrp* 4E **49**
Longframlington. *Nmbd* 2D **9**
Long Green. *Ches* 1C **48**
Longhirst. *Nmbd* 4E **9**
Longhorsley. *Nmbd* 3D **9**
Longhoughton. *Nmbd* 1E **9**
Longlands. *Cumb* 1D **17**
Longlane. *Derbs* 4E **51**
Long Lease. *N Yor* 4C **22**
Long Marston. *N Yor* 1B **36**
Long Marton. *Cumb* 2B **18**
Longmoss. *Ches* 1A **50**
Long Newton. *Stoc T* 3C **20**
Longnor. *Staf* 2C **50**
Longpark. *Cumb* 2F **11**
Long Preston. *N Yor* 1A **34**
Longridge. *Lanc* 3E **33**
Long Riston. *E Yor* 2B **38**
Longsdon. *Staf* 3B **50**
Longshaw. *G Man* 2D **41**
Longshaw. *Staf* 4C **50**
Longslow. *Shrp* 4E **49**
Longthwaite. *Cumb* 2F **17**
Longton. *Lanc* 4C **32**
Longton. *Stoke* 4B **50**
Longtown. *Cumb* 2E **11**
Longwitton. *Nmbd* 4C **8**
Lorbottle. *Nmbd* 2C **8**
Lorbottle Hall. *Nmbd* 2C **8**
Loscoe. *Derbs* 4A **52**
Lostock Gralam. *Ches* 1E **49**
Lostock Green. *Ches* 1E **49**
Lostock Hall. *Lanc* 4D **33**
Lostock Junction. *G Man* 2E **41**
Lothersdale. *N Yor* 2B **34**
Lound. *Notts* 4C **44**
Louth. *Linc* 4D **47**
Love Clough. *Lanc* 4A **34**
Loversall. *S Yor* 3B **44**
Low Ackworth. *W Yor* 1A **44**
Low Angerton. *Nmbd* 4C **8**
Low Barlings. *Linc* 1A **54**
Low Bell End. *N Yor* 1A **30**
Low Bentham. *N Yor* 4B **26**
Low Borrowbridge. *Cumb* 4B **18**
Low Bradfield. *S Yor* 3E **43**
Low Bradley. *N Yor* 2C **34**
Low Braithwaite. *Cumb* 4F **11**
Low Brunton. *Nmbd* 1E **13**
Low Burnham. *N Lin* 2D **45**
Lowca. *Cumb* 2A **16**
Low Catton. *E Yor* 1D **37**
Low Coniscliffe. *Dur* 3B **20**
Low Crosby. *Cumb* 3F **11**
Low Dalby. *N Yor* 2B **30**
Lowdham. *Notts* 4C **52**
Low Dinsdale. *Darl* 3C **20**
Low Ellington. *N Yor* 2B **28**
Lower Ballam. *Lanc* 3B **32**
Lower Cumberworth. *W Yor* 2E **43**
Lower Darwen. *Bkbn* 4E **33**
Lower Dunsforth. *N Yor* 4D **29**
Lower Ellastone. *Derbs* 4D **51**
Lower Hartshay. *Derbs* 3F **51**
Lower Hawthwaite. *Cumb* 2D **25**
Lower Heysham. *Lanc* 4F **25**
Lower Kinnerton. *Ches* 2B **48**
Lower Leigh. *Staf* 4C **50**
Lower Mountain. *Flin* 3B **48**
Lower Peover. *Ches* 1F **49**
Lower Place. *G Man* 1B **42**
Lower Tean. *Staf* 4C **50**
Lower Thurnham. *Lanc* 1C **32**
Lower Thurvaston. *Derbs* 4E **51**
Lower Walton. *Warr* 4E **41**
Lower Whitley. *Ches* 1E **49**
Lower Withington. *Ches* 2A **50**
Lower Wych. *Ches* 4C **48**
Loweswater. *Cumb* 2C **16**
Low Etherley. *Dur* 2A **20**
Low Gate. *Nmbd* 2E **13**
Lowgill. *Cumb* 1B **26**
Lowgill. *Lanc* 4B **26**
Low Grantley. *N Yor* 3B **28**
Low Green. *N Yor* 1E **35**
Low Hameringham. *Linc* 2D **55**
Low Hawkser. *N Yor* 4C **22**
Low Hesket. *Cumb* 4F **11**
Low Hesleyhurst. *Nmbd* 3C **8**
Lowick. *Cumb* 2D **25**
Lowick. *Nmbd* 3C **4**
Lowick Bridge. *Cumb* 2D **25**
Lowick Green. *Cumb* 2D **25**
Low Knipe. *Cumb* 2A **18**
Low Leighton. *Derbs* 4C **42**
Low Lorton. *Cumb* 2C **16**
Low Marishes. *N Yor* 3B **30**
Low Marnham. *Notts* 2E **53**
Low Mill. *N Yor* 1F **29**
Low Moor. *Lanc* 2F **33**
Low Moor. *W Yor* 4D **35**
Low Moorsley. *Tyne* 4C **14**
Low Newton-by-the-Sea. *Nmbd* 4E **5**
Low Row. *Cumb* 2A **12** (nr. Brampton)
Low Row. *Cumb* 4C **10** (nr. Wigton)
Low Row. *N Yor* 1E **27**
Low Team. *Tyne* 2B **14**
Lowther. *Cumb* 2A **18**
Lowthorpe. *E Yor* 4D **31**
Lowton. *G Man* 3E **41**
Lowton Common. *G Man* 3E **41**
Low Toynton. *Linc* 1C **54**
Low Walworth. *Darl* 3B **20**
Low Westwood. *Dur* 3A **14**
Low Whinnow. *Cumb* 3E **11**
Low Wood. *Cumb* 2E **25**
Low Worsall. *N Yor* 4C **20**
Low Wray. *Cumb* 4E **17**
Loxley. *S Yor* 4F **43**
Lucker. *Nmbd* 3D **5**
Ludborough. *Linc* 3C **46**
Luddenden. *W Yor* 4C **34**
Luddenden Foot. *W Yor* 4C **34**
Ludderburn. *Cumb* 1F **25**
Luddington. *N Lin* 1E **45**
Ludford. *Linc* 4B **46**
Ludworth. *Dur* 4C **14**
Lumb. *Lanc* 4A **34**
Lumb. *W Yor* 4C **34**
Lumby. *N Yor* 3A **36**
Lund. *E Yor* 2F **37**
Lund. *N Yor* 3C **36**
Lunt. *Mers* 2B **40**
Lupset. *W Yor* 1F **43**
Lupton. *Cumb* 2A **26**
Lusby. *Linc* 2D **55**
Lydgate. *G Man* 2B **42**
Lydgate. *W Yor* 4B **34**
Lydiate. *Mers* 2B **40**
Lyham. *Nmbd* 3C **4**
Lymm. *Warr* 4E **41**
Lyneal. *Shrp* 4C **48**
Lyneholmeford. *Cumb* 1A **12**
Lynemouth. *Nmbd* 3E **9**
Lynesack. *Dur* 2F **19**
Lytham. *Lanc* 4B **32**
Lytham St Anne's. *Lanc* 4B **32**
Lythe. *N Yor* 3B **22**

M

Mabie. *Dum* 1A **10**
Mablethorpe. *Linc* 4F **47**
Macclesfield. *Ches* 1B **50**
Macclesfield Forest. *Ches* 1B **50**
Mackworth. *Derb* 4F **51**
Madeley. *Staf* 4F **49**
Madeley Heath. *Staf* 4F **49**
Maer. *Staf* 4F **49**
Maes-glas. *Flin* 1A **48**
Maeshafn. *Den* 2A **48**
Maghull. *Mers* 2B **40**
Maiden Law. *Dur* 4A **14**
Maidenwell. *Linc* 1D **55**
Mainsforth. *Dur* 1C **20**
Mainsriddle. *Dum* 3A **10**
Makeney. *Derbs* 4F **51**

Malcoff—New Boultham

Malcoff. *Derbs* 4C 42
Malham. *N Yor* 4E 27
Malpas. *Ches* 4C 48
Maltby. *S Yor* 3B 44
Maltby. *Stoc T* 3D 21
Maltby le Marsh. *Linc* 4E 47
Malton. *N Yor* 3A 30
Manby. *Linc* 4D 47
Manchester. *G Man* 3A 42
Manchester Airport. *G Man* 4A 42
Mancot. *Flin* 2B 48
Manfield. *N Yor* 3B 20
Mankinholes. *W Yor* 4B 34
Manley. *Ches* 1D 49
Manningham. *W Yor* 3D 35
Mansergh. *Cumb* 2B 26
Mansfield. *Notts* 2B 52
Mansfield Woodhouse. *Notts* 2B 52
Mansriggs. *Cumb* 2D 25
Manston. *W Yor* 3F 35
Manthorpe. *Linc* 4F 53
Manton. *N Lin* 2F 45
Manton. *Notts* 1B 52
Maplebeck. *Notts* 2D 53
Mapleton. *Derbs* 4D 51
Mapperley. *Derbs* 4A 52
Mapperley. *Notts* 4B 52
Mapperley Park. *Notts* 4B 52
Mappleton. *E Yor* 2C 38
Mapplewell. *S Yor* 2F 43
Marbury. *Ches* 4D 49
Marchwiel. *Wrex* 4B 48
Mareham le Fen. *Linc* 2C 54
Mareham on the Hill. *Linc* 2C 54
Marehay. *Derbs* 4F 51
Marfleet. *Hull* 4B 38
Marford. *Wrex* 3B 48
Marjoriebanks. *Dum* 1B 10
Markby. *Linc* 1E 55
Markeaton. *Derbs* 4F 51
Market Drayton. *Shrp* 4E 49
Market Rasen. *Linc* 4B 46
Market Stainton. *Linc* 1C 54
Market Warsop. *Notts* 2B 52
Market Weighton. *E Yor* 2E 37
Markington. *N Yor* 4B 28
Marley Green. *Ches* 4D 49
Marley Hill. *Tyne* 3B 14
Marlpool. *Derbs* 4A 52
Marple. *G Man* 4B 42
Marr. *S Yor* 2B 44
Marrick. *N Yor* 1F 27
Marsden. *Tyne* 2C 14
Marsden. *W Yor* 1C 42
Marsett. *N Yor* 2E 27
Marshall Meadows. *Nmbd* 1B 4
Marshaw. *Lanc* 1D 33
Marshchapel. *Linc* 3D 47
Marsh Green. *Staf* 3A 50
Marsh Lane. *Derbs* 1A 52
Marshside. *Mers* 1B 40
Marske. *N Yor* 4A 20
Marske-by-the-Sea. *Red C* 2F 21
Marston. *Ches* 1E 49
Marston. *Notts* 4E 53
Marston Montgomery. *Derbs* 4D 51
Marthall. *Ches* 1A 50
Marthwaite. *Cumb* 1B 26
Martin. *Linc* 2C 54 (nr. Horncastle)
Martin. *Linc* 3B 54 (nr. Metheringham)
Martindale. *Cumb* 3F 17
Martin Dales. *Linc* 2B 54
Martinscroft. *Warr* 4E 41
Martin's Moss. *Ches* 2A 50
Marton. *Ches* 2A 50
Marton. *Cumb* 3D 25
Marton. *E Yor* 4F 31 (nr. Bridlington)
Marton. *E Yor* 3B 38 (nr. Hull)
Marton. *Linc* 4E 45
Marton. *Midd* 3E 21
Marton. *N Yor* 4D 29 (nr. Boroughbridge)
Marton. *N Yor* 2A 30 (nr. Pickering)
Marton Abbey. *N Yor* 4E 29
Marton-le-Moor. *N Yor* 3C 28
Marylebone. *G Man* 2D 41
Maryport. *Cumb* 1B 16
Masham. *N Yor* 2B 28
Masongill. *N Yor* 3B 26
Mastin Moor. *Derbs* 1A 52
Matfen. *Nmbd* 1F 13
Matlock. *Derbs* 2E 51
Matlock Bath. *Derbs* 3E 51
Matterdale End. *Cumb* 2E 17
Mattersey. *Notts* 4C 44
Mattersey Thorpe. *Notts* 4C 44
Maulds Meaburn. *Cumb* 3B 18
Maunby. *N Yor* 2C 28
Mavis Enderby. *Linc* 2D 55
Mawbray. *Cumb* 4B 10
Mawdesley. *Lanc* 1C 40
Maw Green. *Ches* 3F 49
Mawthorpe. *Linc* 1E 55
Maxwelltown. *Dum* 1A 10
Mayfield. *Staf* 4D 51
Meadowbank. *Ches* 2E 49
Meadowfield. *Dur* 1B 20
Meadows. *Nott* 4B 52
Meal Bank. *Cumb* 1A 26
Mealrigg. *Cumb* 4C 10
Mealsgate. *Cumb* 4D 11
Meanwood. *W Yor* 3E 35
Mearbeck. *N Yor* 4D 27
Meathop. *Cumb* 2F 25
Meaux. *E Yor* 3A 38
Medburn. *Nmbd* 1A 14
Meden Vale. *Notts* 2B 52
Medlam. *Linc* 3D 55
Medomsley. *Dur* 3A 14
Meerbrook. *Staf* 2B 50
Meers Bridge. *Linc* 4E 47
Meir. *Stoke* 4B 50
Meir Heath. *Staf* 4B 50
Melbourne. *E Yor* 2D 37
Meldon. *Nmbd* 4D 9
Melkington. *Nmbd* 2A 4
Melkinthorpe. *Cumb* 2A 18
Melkridge. *Nmbd* 2C 12
Mellguards. *Cumb* 4F 11
Melling. *Lanc* 3A 26
Melling. *Mers* 2B 40
Melling Mount. *Mers* 2C 40
Mellor. *G Man* 4B 42
Mellor. *Lanc* 3E 33
Mellor Brook. *Lanc* 3E 33
Melmerby. *Cumb* 1B 18
Melmerby. *N Yor* 2F 27 (nr. Middleham)
Melmerby. *N Yor* 3C 28 (nr. Ripon)
Melsonby. *N Yor* 4A 20
Meltham. *W Yor* 1C 42
Meltham Mills. *W Yor* 1D 43
Melton. *E Yor* 4F 37
Meltonby. *E Yor* 1D 37
Melton Ross. *N Lin* 1A 46
Menethorpe. *N Yor* 4A 30
Menston. *W Yor* 2D 35
Menthorpe. *N Yor* 3D 37
Meols. *Mers* 4A 40
Mercaston. *Derbs* 4E 51
Mere. *Ches* 4F 41
Mere Brow. *Lanc* 1C 40
Mereclough. *Lanc* 3A 34
Mere Heath. *Ches* 1E 49
Mereside. *Bkpl* 3B 32
Merrybent. *Darl* 3B 20
Messingham. *N Lin* 2E 45
Metheringham. *Linc* 2A 54
Methley. *W Yor* 4F 35
Methley Junction. *W Yor* 4F 35
Mexborough. *S Yor* 2A 44
Micklebring. *S Yor* 3B 44
Mickleby. *N Yor* 3B 22
Micklefield. *W Yor* 3A 36
Mickleover. *Derb* 4F 51
Micklethwaite. *Cumb* 3D 11
Micklethwaite. *W Yor* 2D 35
Mickleton. *Dur* 2E 19
Mickletown. *W Yor* 4F 35
Mickle Trafford. *Ches* 2C 48
Mickley. *N Yor* 3B 28
Mickley Square. *Nmbd* 2F 13
Middlebie. *Dum* 1D 11
Middlecliff. *S Yor* 2A 44
Middleforth Green. *Lanc* 4D 33
Middleham. *N Yor* 2A 28
Middle Handley. *Derbs* 1A 52
Middle Mayfield. *Staf* 4D 51
Middle Rainton. *Tyne* 4C 14
Middle Rasen. *Linc* 4A 46
Middlesbrough. *Midd* 2D 21
Middlesceugh. *Cumb* 4E 11
Middleshaw. *Cumb* 2A 26
Middlesmoor. *N Yor* 3F 27
Middles, The. *Dur* 3B 14
Middlestone. *Dur* 1B 20
Middlestone Moor. *Dur* 1B 20
Middlestown. *W Yor* 1E 43
Middleton. *Cumb* 2B 26
Middleton. *Derbs* 2D 51 (nr. Bakewell)
Middleton. *Derbs* 3E 51 (nr. Wirksworth)
Middleton. *G Man* 2A 42
Middleton. *Hart* 1E 21
Middleton. *Lanc* 1C 32
Middleton. *Nmbd* 3D 5 (nr. Belford)
Middleton. *Nmbd* 4C 8 (nr. Morpeth)
Middleton. *N Yor* 2D 35 (nr. Ilkley)
Middleton. *N Yor* 2A 30 (nr. Pickering)
Middleton. *W Yor* 4F 35
Middleton Green. *Staf* 4B 50
Middleton Hall. *Nmbd* 4B 4
Middleton in Teesdale. *Dur* 2E 19
Middleton One Row. *Darl* 3C 20
Middleton-on-Leven. *N Yor* 4D 21
Middleton-on-the-Wolds. *E Yor* 2F 37
Middleton Quernhow. *N Yor* 3C 28
Middleton St George. *Darl* 3C 20
Middleton Tyas. *N Yor* 4B 20
Middletown. *Cumb* 4A 16
Middlewich. *Ches* 2F 49
Middlewood. *S Yor* 3F 43
Middridge. *Dur* 2B 20
Midge Hall. *Lanc* 4D 33
Midgeholme. *Cumb* 3B 12
Midgley. *W Yor* 4C 34 (nr. Halifax)
Midgley. *W Yor* 1E 43 (nr. Horbury)
Midhopestones. *S Yor* 3E 43
Midville. *Linc* 3D 55
Milbourne. *Nmbd* 1A 14
Milburn. *Cumb* 2B 18
Milby. *N Yor* 4D 29
Miles Green. *Staf* 3A 50
Milfield. *Nmbd* 3B 4
Milford. *Derbs* 4F 51
Mill Bank. *W Yor* 4C 34
Millbeck. *Cumb* 2D 17
Millbrook. *G Man* 3B 42
Milldale. *Staf* 3D 51
Miller's Dale. *Derbs* 1D 51
Millers Green. *Derbs* 3E 51
Millgate. *Lanc* 1A 42
Millhead. *Lanc* 3F 25
Mill Hill. *Bkbn* 4E 33
Millholme. *Cumb* 1A 26
Millhousebridge. *Dum* 1C 10
Millhouses. *S Yor* 4F 43
Millington. *E Yor* 1E 37
Millington Green. *Derbs* 4E 51
Millmeece. *Staf* 4A 50
Millom. *Cumb* 2C 24
Mill Side. *Cumb* 2F 25
Millthorpe. *Derbs* 1F 51
Millthrop. *Cumb* 1B 26
Milltown. *Derbs* 2F 51
Milltown. *Dum* 1E 11
Milnrow. *G Man* 1B 42
Milnthorpe. *Cumb* 2F 25
Milnthorpe. *W Yor* 1F 43
Milton. *Cumb* 2A 12
Milton. *Dum* 1A 10
Milton. *Notts* 1D 53
Milton. *Stoke* 3B 50
Milton Green. *Ches* 3C 48
Mindrum. *Nmbd* 3A 4
Minera. *Wrex* 3A 48
Miningsby. *Linc* 2D 55
Minskip. *N Yor* 4C 28
Minsteracres. *Nmbd* 3F 13
Minting. *Linc* 1B 54
Minto. *Scot* 1D 7
Mirehouse. *Cumb* 3A 16
Mirfield. *W Yor* 1E 43
Misson. *Notts* 3C 44
Misterton. *Notts* 3D 45
Mitford. *Nmbd* 4D 9
Mixenden. *W Yor* 4C 34
Mixon. *Staf* 3C 50
Moat. *Cumb* 1F 11
Mobberley. *Ches* 1F 49
Mobberley. *Staf* 4C 50
Mockerkin. *Cumb* 2B 16
Moddershall. *Staf* 4B 50
Mold. *Flin* 2A 48
Molescroft. *E Yor* 2A 38
Molesden. *Nmbd* 4D 9
Mollington. *Ches* 1B 48
Monk Bretton. *S Yor* 2F 43
Monk Fryston. *N Yor* 4B 36
Monk Hesleden. *Dur* 1D 21
Monkhill. *Cumb* 3E 11
Monkseaton. *Tyne* 1C 14
Monk's Heath. *Ches* 1A 50
Monksthorpe. *Linc* 2E 55
Monkwearmouth. *Tyne* 3D 15
Monyash. *Derbs* 2D 51
Moor Allerton. *W Yor* 3F 35
Moorby. *Linc* 2C 54
Moore. *Hal* 4D 41
Moorend. *Dum* 1D 11
Moor End. *E Yor* 3E 37
Moorends. *S Yor* 1C 44
Moorgate. *S Yor* 3A 44
Moorgreen. *Notts* 4A 52
Moorhaigh. *Notts* 2B 52
Moorhall. *Derbs* 1F 51
Moorhouse. *Cumb* 3E 11 (nr. Carlisle)
Moorhouse. *Cumb* 3D 11 (nr. Wigton)
Moorhouse. *Notts* 2D 53
Moorhouses. *Linc* 3C 54
Moor Monkton. *N Yor* 1B 36
Moor Row. *Cumb* 3B 16 (nr. Whitehaven)
Moor Row. *Cumb* 4D 11 (nr. Wigton)
Moorsholm. *Red C* 3F 21
Moorside. *G Man* 2B 42
Moortown. *Linc* 3A 46
Moortown. *W Yor* 3F 35
Mordon. *Dur* 2C 20
Morebattle. *Scot* 4A 4
Morecambe. *Lanc* 4F 25
Moresby Parks. *Cumb* 3A 16
Moreton. *Mers* 3A 40
Moreton Say. *Shrp* 4E 49
Morland. *Cumb* 2A 18
Morley. *Ches* 4A 42
Morley. *Derbs* 4F 51
Morley. *Dur* 2A 20
Morley. *W Yor* 4E 35
Morpeth. *Nmbd* 4E 9
Morridge Side. *Staf* 3C 50
Morridge Top. *Staf* 2C 50
Morrington. *Dum* 1A 10
Morthen. *S Yor* 4A 44
Mortomley. *S Yor* 3F 43
Morton. *Cumb* 1F 17 (nr. Calthwaite)
Morton. *Cumb* 3E 11 (nr. Carlisle)
Morton. *Derbs* 2A 52
Morton. *Linc* 3E 45 (nr. Gainsborough)
Morton. *Linc* 2E 53 (nr. Lincoln)
Morton. *Notts* 3D 53
Morton-on-Swale. *N Yor* 1C 28
Morton Tinmouth. *Dur* 2A 20
Morwick Hall. *Nmbd* 2E 9
Mosborough. *S Yor* 4A 44
Mosedale. *Cumb* 1E 17
Moss. *S Yor* 1B 44
Moss. *Wrex* 3B 48
Moss Bank. *Mers* 3D 41
Mossbrow. *G Man* 4F 41
Mossburnford. *Scot* 1E 7
Mossedge. *Cumb* 2F 11
Mossgate. *Staf* 4B 50
Moss Lane. *Ches* 1B 50
Mossley. *Ches* 2A 50
Mossley. *G Man* 2B 42
Mossley Hill. *Mers* 4B 40
Mosspaul. *Scot* 3C 6
Moss Side. *Cumb* 3C 10
Moss Side. *G Man* 3A 42
Moss Side. *Lanc* 3B 32 (nr. Blackpool)
Moss Side. *Lanc* 4D 33 (nr. Preston)
Moss Side. *Mers* 2B 40
Mosswood. *Nmbd* 3F 13
Mossy Lea. *Lanc* 1D 41
Mossy Green. *Ches* 2F 49
Mostyn. *Flin* 4A 40
Motherby. *Cumb* 2F 17
Mottram in Longdendale. *G Man* 3B 42
Mottram St Andrew. *Ches* 1A 50
Mouldsworth. *Ches* 1D 49
Moulton. *Ches* 2E 49
Moulton. *N Yor* 4B 20
Mountbenger. *Scot* 1B 6
Mount Pleasant. *Ches* 3A 50
Mount Pleasant. *Derbs* 4F 51
Mouswald. *Dum* 1B 10
Mow Cop. *Staf* 3A 50
Mowden. *Darl* 3B 20
Mowhaugh. *Scot* 4A 4
Much Hoole. *Lanc* 4C 32
Mucklestone. *Staf* 4F 49
Muckton. *Linc* 4D 47
Muggington. *Derbs* 4E 51
Muggintonlane End. *Derbs* 4E 51
Muggleswick. *Dur* 3F 13
Muker. *N Yor* 1E 27
Mumby. *Linc* 1F 55
Mungrisdale. *Cumb* 1E 17
Murdishaw. *Hal* 4D 41
Murton. *Cumb* 2C 18
Murton. *Dur* 4C 14
Murton. *Nmbd* 2B 4
Murton. *York* 1C 36
Muscoates. *N Yor* 2F 29
Muston. *Leics* 4E 53
Muston. *N Yor* 3D 31
Myerscough. *Lanc* 3C 32
Mynydd Isa. *Flin* 2A 48
Mytholmroyd. *W Yor* 4C 34
Myton-on-Swale. *N Yor* 4D 29

N

Naburn. *York* 2B 36
Nab Wood. *W Yor* 3D 35
Nafferton. *E Yor* 1A 38
Naisberry. *Hart* 1D 21
Nangreaves. *G Man* 1A 42
Nannerch. *Flin* 2A 48
Nantwich. *Ches* 3E 49
Nappa. *N Yor* 1A 34
Narthwaite. *Cumb* 1C 26
Nateby. *Cumb* 4C 18
Nateby. *Lanc* 2C 32
Natland. *Cumb* 2A 26
Navenby. *Linc* 3F 53
Nawton. *N Yor* 2F 29
Neap House. *N Lin* 1E 45
Near Sawrey. *Cumb* 1E 25
Neasham. *Darl* 3C 20
Nedderton. *Nmbd* 4E 9
Nelson. *Lanc* 3A 34
Nelson Village. *Nmbd* 1B 14
Nenthall. *Cumb* 4C 12
Nenthead. *Cumb* 4C 12
Nercwys. *Flin* 2A 48
Nesbit. *Nmbd* 3B 4
Nesfield. *N Yor* 2C 34
Ness. *Ches* 1B 48
Neston. *Ches* 1A 48
Nether Alderley. *Ches* 1A 50
Nether Burrow. *Lanc* 3B 26
Netherby. *Cumb* 1E 11
Nether End. *Derbs* 1E 51
Netherfield. *Notts* 4C 52
Nether Handley. *Derbs* 1A 52
Nether Haugh. *S Yor* 3A 44
Nether Heage. *Derbs* 3F 51
Netherhouses. *Cumb* 2D 25
Nether Kellet. *Lanc* 4A 26
Nether Langwith. *Notts* 2B 52
Nether Moor. *Derbs* 2F 51
Nether Padley. *Derbs* 1E 51
Nether Poppleton. *York* 1B 36
Nether Silton. *N Yor* 1D 29
Netherthong. *W Yor* 2D 43
Netherton. *Cumb* 1B 16
Netherton. *Mers* 3B 40
Netherton. *Nmbd* 2B 8
Netherton. *W Yor* 1E 43 (nr. Horbury)
Netherton. *W Yor* 1D 43 (nr. Huddersfield)
Nethertown. *Cumb* 4A 16
Nether Wasdale. *Cumb* 4C 16
Nether Welton. *Cumb* 4E 11
Netherwhitton. *Nmbd* 3D 9
Nettleham. *Linc* 1A 54
Nettlesworth. *Dur* 4B 14
Nettleton. *Linc* 2B 46
New Abbey. *Dum* 2A 10
Newall. *W Yor* 2D 35
Newark-on-Trent. *Notts* 3D 53
New Balderton. *Notts* 3E 53
New Barnetby. *N Lin* 1A 46
New Bewick. *Nmbd* 4C 4
Newbiggin. *Cumb* 2B 18 (nr. Appleby)
Newbiggin. *Cumb* 4D 25 (nr. Barrow-in-Furness)
Newbiggin. *Cumb* 4A 12 (nr. Cumrew)
Newbiggin. *Cumb* 2F 17 (nr. Penrith)
Newbiggin. *Cumb* 1B 24 (nr. Seascale)
Newbiggin. *Dur* 4A 14 (nr. Consett)
Newbiggin. *Dur* 2E 19 (nr. Holwick)
Newbiggin. *Nmbd* 4E 13
Newbiggin. *N Yor* 1E 27 (nr. Askrigg)
Newbiggin. *N Yor* 2E 31 (nr. Filey)
Newbiggin. *N Yor* 2E 27 (nr. Thoralby)
Newbiggin-by-the-Sea. *Nmbd* 4F 9
Newbiggin-on-Lune. *Cumb* 4C 18
Newbold. *Derbs* 1F 51
New Bolingbroke. *Linc* 3D 55
Newbottle. *Tyne* 3C 14
New Boultham. *Linc* 1F 53

Northern England Regional Atlas 65

New Brancepeth—Pardshaw

New Brancepeth. *Dur* 4B 14
New Bridge. *Dum* 1A 10
Newbridge. *N Yor* 2B 30
Newbridge. *Wrex* 4A 48
New Brighton. *Flin* 2A 48
New Brinsley. *Notts* 3A 52
Newbrough. *Nmbd* 2D 13
New Broughton. *Wrex* 3B 48
Newburgh. *Lanc* 1C 40
Newburn. *Tyne* 2A 14
Newby. *Cumb* 2A 18
Newby. *N Yor* 3C 26 (nr. Ingleton)
Newby. *N Yor* 2D 31 (nr. Scarborough)
Newby. *N Yor* 3E 21 (nr. Stokesley)
Newby Bridge. *Cumb* 2E 25
Newby Cote. *N Yor* 3C 26
Newby East. *Cumb* 3F 11
Newby Head. *Cumb* 2A 18
Newby West. *Cumb* 3E 11
Newby Wiske. *N Yor* 2C 28
Newcastle Airport. *Tyne* 1A 14
Newcastleton. *Scot* 4C 6
Newcastle-under-Lyme. *Staf* 4A 50
Newcastle upon Tyne. *Tyne* 2B 14
Newchapel. *Staf* 3A 50
Newchurch. *Lanc* 3A 34 (nr. Nelson)
Newchurch. *Lanc* 4A 34 (nr. Rawtenstall)
New Cowper. *Cumb* 4C 10
New Crofton. *W Yor* 1F 43
New Earswick. *York* 1C 36
New Edlington. *S Yor* 3B 44
New Ellerby. *E Yor* 3B 38
New Ferry. *Mers* 4B 40
Newfield. *Dur* 3B 14 (nr. Chester-le-Street)
Newfield. *Dur* 1B 20 (nr. Willington)
New Fryston. *W Yor* 4A 36
Newhall. *Ches* 4E 49
Newham. *Nmbd* 4D 5
New Hartley. *Nmbd* 1C 14
Newhaven. *Derbs* 2D 51
New Herrington. *Tyne* 3C 14
Newhey. *G Man* 1B 42
New Holland. *N Lin* 4A 38
Newholm. *N Yor* 3B 22
New Houghton. *Derbs* 2B 52
New Houses. *N Yor* 3D 27
New Hutton. *Cumb* 1A 26
Newington. *Notts* 3C 44
New Inn. *N Yor* 3D 27
Newland. *Hull* 3A 38
Newland. *N Yor* 4C 36
Newlands. *Cumb* 1E 17
Newlands. *Nmbd* 3F 13
Newlands. *Notts* 2B 52
New Lane. *Lanc* 1C 40
New Lane End. *Warr* 3E 41
New Langholm. *Dum* 4B 6
New Leake. *Linc* 3E 55
New Longton. *Lanc* 4D 33
New Marske. *Red C* 2F 21
New Marton. *Shrp* 4B 48
Newmill. *Scot* 1C 6
New Mill. *W Yor* 2D 43
Newmillerdam. *W Yor* 1F 43
New Mills. *Derbs* 4C 42
New Ollerton. *Notts* 2C 52
New Park. *N Yor* 1E 35
Newport. *E Yor* 3E 37
New Rent. *Cumb* 1F 17
New Ridley. *Nmbd* 3F 13
New Rossington. *S Yor* 3C 44
New Row. *Lanc* 3E 33
New Row. *N Yor* 3F 21
Newsbank. *Ches* 2A 50
Newsham. *Lanc* 3D 33
Newsham. *Nmbd* 1C 14
Newsham. *N Yor* 3A 20 (nr. Richmond)
Newsham. *N Yor* 2C 28 (nr. Thirsk)
New Sharlston. *W Yor* 1F 43
Newsholme. *E Yor* 4D 37
Newsholme. *Lanc* 1A 34
New Shoreston. *Nmbd* 3D 5
New Springs. *G Man* 2E 41
Newstead. *Notts* 3B 52
Newstreet Lane. *Shrp* 4E 49
Newthorpe. *N Yor* 3A 36
Newthorpe. *Notts* 4A 52
Newton. *Ches* 2C 48 (nr. Chester)
Newton. *Ches* 3D 49 (nr. Tattenhall)
Newton. *Cumb* 3D 25
Newton. *Derbs* 3A 52
Newton. *Dum* 1D 11
Newton. *G Man* 3B 42
Newton. *Lanc* 3A 26 (nr. Carnforth)
Newton. *Lanc* 1F 33 (nr. Clitheroe)
Newton. *Lanc* 3C 32 (nr. Kirkham)
Newton. *Linc* 4A 54
Newton. *Mers* 4A 40
Newton. *Nmbd* 2F 13
Newton. *Notts* 4C 52
Newton. *Scot* 1E 7
Newton. *Shrp* 4C 48
Newtonairds. *Dum* 1A 10
Newton Arlosh. *Cumb* 3D 11
Newton Aycliffe. *Dur* 2B 20
Newton Bewley. *Hart* 2D 21
Newton by Toft. *Linc* 4A 46
Newton Hall. *Dur* 4B 14
Newton Hall. *Nmbd* 2F 13
Newton Heath. *G Man* 2A 42
Newton Hill. *W Yor* 4F 35
Newton Ketton. *Darl* 2C 20
Newton Kyme. *N Yor* 2A 36
Newton-le-Willows. *Mers* 3D 41
Newton-le-Willows. *N Yor* 2B 28
Newton Morrell. *N Yor* 4B 20
Newton Mulgrave. *N Yor* 3A 22
Newton-on-Ouse. *N Yor* 4E 29
Newton-on-Rawcliffe. *N Yor* 1B 30
Newton-on-the-Moor. *Nmbd* 2D 9
Newton on Trent. *Linc* 1E 53
Newton Reigny. *Cumb* 1F 17
Newton Rigg. *Cumb* 1F 17
Newton under Roseberry. *Red C* 3E 21
Newton upon Derwent. *E Yor* 2D 37
Newton with Scales. *Lanc* 3B 32
Newtown. *Ches* 4E 49
Newtown. *Cumb* 4B 10 (nr. Aspatria)
Newtown. *Cumb* 2A 12 (nr. Brampton)
Newtown. *Cumb* 2A 18 (nr. Penrith)
Newtown. *Derbs* 4B 42
Newtown. *Lanc* 1D 41
Newtown. *Nmbd* 2C 8 (nr. Rothbury)
Newtown. *Nmbd* 4C 4 (nr. Wooler)
Newtown. *Staf* 2B 50 (nr. Biddulph)
Newtown. *Staf* 2C 50 (nr. Longnor)
New Town. *W Yor* 4A 36
New Village. *E Yor* 3A 38
New Village. *S Yor* 2B 44
New Waltham. *NE Lin* 2C 46
New York. *Linc* 3C 54
New York. *Tyne* 1C 14
Nidd. *N Yor* 4C 28
Ninebanks. *Nmbd* 3C 12
Nisbet. *Scot* 1E 7
Nisbet Hill. *Scot* 1A 4
Nocton. *Linc* 2A 54
No Man's Heath. *Ches* 4D 49
Nook. *Cumb* 1F 11 (nr. Longtown)
Nook. *Cumb* 2A 26 (nr. Milnthorpe)
Norbreck. *Bkpl* 2B 32
Norbury. *Ches* 4D 49
Norbury. *Derbs* 4D 51
Norby. *N Yor* 2D 29
Norcross. *Lanc* 2B 32
Norden. *G Man* 1A 42
Norham. *Nmbd* 2B 4
Norland Town. *W Yor* 4C 34
Norley. *Ches* 1D 49
Normanby. *N Lin* 1E 45
Normanby. *N Yor* 2A 30
Normanby. *Red C* 3E 21
Normanby-by-Spital. *Linc* 4A 46
Normanby le Wold. *Linc* 3B 46
Normanton. *Leics* 4E 53
Normanton. *Linc* 4F 53
Normanton. *Notts* 3D 53
Normanton. *W Yor* 4F 35
Normanton on Trent. *Notts* 2D 53
Normoss. *Lanc* 3B 32
Norris Green. *Mers* 3B 40
Norristhorpe. *W Yor* 4E 35
Northallerton. *N Yor* 1C 28
North Anston. *S Yor* 4B 44
Northbeck. *Linc* 4A 54
North Bitchburn. *Dur* 1A 20
North Blyth. *Nmbd* 4F 9
North Carlton. *Linc* 1F 53
North Cave. *E Yor* 3E 37
North Charlton. *Nmbd* 4D 5
North Cliffe. *E Yor* 3E 37
North Clifton. *Notts* 1E 53
North Close. *Dur* 1B 20
North Cockerington. *Linc* 3D 47
North Corbelly. *Dum* 2A 10
North Cotes. *Linc* 2D 47
North Cowton. *N Yor* 4B 20
North Dalton. *E Yor* 1F 37
North Deighton. *N Yor* 1F 35
North Duffield. *N Yor* 3C 36
Northedge. *Derbs* 2F 51
North Elkington. *Linc* 3C 46
North Elmsall. *W Yor* 1A 44
North End. *E Yor* 3C 38
North End. *Linc* 4C 54
North Featherstone. *W Yor* 4A 36
North Ferriby. *E Yor* 4F 37
Northfield. *E Yor* 4A 38
North Frodingham. *E Yor* 1B 38
North Greetwell. *Linc* 1A 54
North Grimston. *N Yor* 4B 30
North Hazelrigg. *Nmbd* 3C 4
North Hykeham. *Linc* 2F 53
North Kelsey. *Linc* 2A 46
North Kelsey Moor. *Linc* 2A 46
North Killingholme. *N Lin* 1B 46
North Kilvington. *N Yor* 2D 29
North Kyme. *Linc* 3B 54
Northlands. *Linc* 3D 55
North Lees. *N Yor* 3C 28
North Leverton with Habblesthorpe. *Notts* 4D 45
North Middleton. *Nmbd* 4C 4
North Moor. *N Yor* 2C 30
North Muskham. *Notts* 3D 53
North Newbald. *E Yor* 3F 37
Northop. *Flin* 2A 48
Northop Hall. *Flin* 2A 48
North Ormesby. *Midd* 2E 21
North Ormsby. *Linc* 3C 46
Northorpe. *Linc* 4C 54 (nr. Donington)
Northorpe. *Linc* 3E 45 (nr. Gainsborough)
North Otterington. *N Yor* 2C 28
North Owersby. *Linc* 3A 46
Northowram. *W Yor* 4D 35
North Rauceby. *Linc* 4A 54
North Rigton. *N Yor* 2E 35
North Rode. *Ches* 2A 50
North Row. *Cumb* 1D 17
North Scale. *Cumb* 4C 24
North Scarle. *Linc* 2E 53
North Seaton. *Nmbd* 4E 9
North Seaton Colliery. *Nmbd* 4E 9
North Shields. *Tyne* 2C 14
North Shore. *Bkpl* 3B 32
North Side. *Cumb* 2B 16
North Skelton. *Red C* 3F 21
North Somercotes. *Linc* 3E 47
North Stainley. *N Yor* 3B 28
North Stainmore. *Cumb* 3D 19
North Sunderland. *Nmbd* 3E 5
North Thoresby. *Linc* 3C 46
North Walbottle. *Tyne* 2A 14
North Wheatley. *Notts* 4D 45
Northwich. *Ches* 1E 49
North Willingham. *Linc* 4B 46
North Wingfield. *Derbs* 2A 52
Northwood. *Derbs* 2E 51
Northwood. *Stoke* 4A 50
North Yardhope. *Nmbd* 2B 8
Norton. *Hal* 4D 41
Norton. *N Yor* 3A 30
Norton. *Notts* 1B 52
Norton. *S Yor* 1B 44 (nr. Askern)
Norton. *S Yor* 4F 43 (nr. Sheffield)
Norton. *Stoc T* 2D 21
Norton Disney. *Linc* 3E 53
Norton Green. *Stoke* 3B 50
Norton in Hales. *Shrp* 4F 49
Norton in the Moors. *Stoke* 3A 50
Norton-le-Clay. *N Yor* 3D 29
Norton Woodseats. *S Yor* 4F 43
Norwell. *Notts* 2D 53
Norwell Woodhouse. *Notts* 2D 53
Norwood. *Derbs* 4A 44
Norwood Green. *W Yor* 4D 35
Nosterfield. *N Yor* 2B 28
Nottingham. *Nott* 4B 52
Notton. *W Yor* 1F 43
Nunburnholme. *E Yor* 2E 37
Nuncargate. *Notts* 3B 52
Nunclose. *Cumb* 4F 11
Nun Monkton. *N Yor* 1B 36
Nunnington. *N Yor* 3F 29
Nunnykirk. *Nmbd* 3C 8
Nunsthorpe. *NE Lin* 2C 46
Nunthorpe. *Midd* 3E 21
Nunthorpe. *York* 2B 36
Nunwick. *Nmbd* 1D 13
Nunwick. *N Yor* 3C 28
Nuthall. *Notts* 4A 52
Nuttall. *G Man* 1F 41
Nutwell. *S Yor* 2C 44

O

Oakamoor. *Staf* 4C 50
Oakenclough. *Lanc* 2D 33
Oakenholt. *Flin* 1A 48
Oakenshaw. *Dur* 1B 20
Oakenshaw. *W Yor* 4D 35
Oakerthorpe. *Derbs* 3F 51
Oakgrove. *Ches* 2B 50
Oakhanger. *Ches* 3F 49
Oakmere. *Ches* 2D 49
Oaks Green. *Derbs* 4D 51
Oakshaw Ford. *Cumb* 1A 12
Oak Tree. *Darl* 3C 20
Oakwood. *Derb* 4F 51
Oakwood. *W Yor* 3F 35
Oakworth. *W Yor* 3C 34
Oasby. *Linc* 4A 54
Oatlands. *N Yor* 1F 35
Occlestone Green. *Ches* 2E 49
Ockbrook. *Derbs* 4A 52
Octon. *E Yor* 4D 31
Offerton. *G Man* 4B 42
Offerton. *Tyne* 3C 14
Ogden. *G Man* 1B 42
Ogle. *Nmbd* 1A 14
Old Barns. *Nmbd* 2E 9
Old Basford. *Nott* 4B 52
Old Bewick. *Nmbd* 4C 4
Old Bolingbroke. *Linc* 2D 55
Old Brampton. *Derbs* 1F 51
Old Byland. *N Yor* 2E 29
Old Cassop. *Dur* 1C 20
Oldcastle Heath. *Ches* 4C 48
Old Clee. *NE Lin* 2C 46
Old Clipstone. *Notts* 2C 52
Oldcotes. *Notts* 4B 44
Old Dam. *Derbs* 1D 51
Old Edlington. *S Yor* 3B 44
Old Eldon. *Dur* 2B 20
Old Ellerby. *E Yor* 3B 38
Old Glossop. *Derbs* 3C 42
Old Goole. *E Yor* 4D 37
Old Graitney. *Dum* 2E 11
Old Hall. *E Yor* 1C 46
Oldham. *G Man* 2B 42
Old Hutton. *Cumb* 2A 26
Old Leake. *Linc* 3E 55
Old Malton. *N Yor* 3A 30
Old Quarrington. *Dur* 1C 20
Old Snydale. *W Yor* 4A 36
Old Somerby. *Linc* 4F 53
Old Spital. *Dur* 3E 19
Oldstead. *N Yor* 2E 29
Old Swan. *Mers* 3B 40
Old Swarland. *Nmbd* 2D 9
Old Tebay. *Cumb* 4B 18
Old Town. *Cumb* 4F 11
Old Town. *Nmbd* 3A 8
Old Trafford. *G Man* 3A 42
Old Tupton. *Derbs* 2F 51
Oldwall. *Cumb* 2F 11
Ollerton. *Ches* 1F 49
Ollerton. *Notts* 2C 52
Ompton. *Notts* 2C 52
Onecote. *Staf* 3C 50
Onneley. *Shrp* 4F 49
Openwoodgate. *Derbs* 4F 51
Orby. *Linc* 2E 55
Ordley. *Nmbd* 3E 13
Ordsall. *Notts* 1D 53
Orford. *Linc* 3C 46
Orford. *Warr* 3E 41
Ormathwaite. *Cumb* 2D 17
Ormesby. *Midd* 3E 21
Ormsgill. *Cumb* 3C 24
Ormskirk. *Lanc* 2C 40
Orrell. *G Man* 2D 41
Orrell. *Mers* 3B 40
Orston. *Notts* 4D 53
Orthwaite. *Cumb* 1D 17
Orton. *Cumb* 4B 18
Osbaldeston. *Lanc* 3E 33
Osbaldwick. *York* 1C 36
Osbournby. *Linc* 4A 54
Oscroft. *Ches* 2D 49
Osgodby. *Linc* 3A 46
Osgodby. *N Yor* 2D 31 (nr. Scarborough)
Osgodby. *N Yor* 3C 36 (nr. Selby)
Osleston. *Derbs* 4E 51
Osmaston. *Derb* 4F 51
Osmaston. *Derbs* 4E 51
Osmondthorpe. *W Yor* 3F 35
Osmotherley. *N Yor* 1D 29
Ossett. *W Yor* 4E 35
Ossington. *Notts* 2D 53
Oswaldkirk. *N Yor* 3F 29
Oswaldtwistle. *Lanc* 4F 33
Otby. *Linc* 3B 46
Otley. *W Yor* 2E 35
Otterburn. *Nmbd* 3A 8
Otterburn. *N Yor* 1A 34
Otterburn Camp. *Nmbd* 3A 8
Otterburn Hall. *Nmbd* 3A 8
Otterspool. *Mers* 4B 40
Ottringham. *E Yor* 4C 38
Oughterby. *Cumb* 3D 11
Oughtershaw. *N Yor* 2D 27
Oughterside. *Cumb* 4C 10
Oughtibridge. *S Yor* 3F 43
Oughtrington. *Warr* 4E 41
Oulston. *N Yor* 3E 29
Oulton. *Cumb* 3D 11
Oulton. *Staf* 4B 50
Oulton. *W Yor* 4F 35
Ousby. *Cumb* 1B 18
Ousefleet. *E Yor* 4E 37
Ouston. *Dur* 3B 14
Ouston. *Nmbd* 3C 12 (nr. Bearsbridge)
Ouston. *Nmbd* 1F 13 (nr. Stamfordham)
Outgate. *Cumb* 4E 17
Outhgill. *Cumb* 4C 18
Outlane. *W Yor* 1C 42
Out Newton. *E Yor* 4D 39
Out Rawcliffe. *Lanc* 2C 32
Outwood. *W Yor* 4F 35
Ouzlewell Green. *W Yor* 4F 35
Ovenden. *W Yor* 4C 34
Over. *Ches* 2E 49
Over Burrows. *Derbs* 4E 51
Overgreen. *Derbs* 1F 51
Over Haddon. *Derbs* 2E 51
Over Hulton. *G Man* 2E 41
Over Kellet. *Lanc* 3A 26
Over Peover. *Ches* 1F 49
Overpool. *Ches* 1B 48
Over Silton. *N Yor* 1D 29
Overton. *Ches* 1D 49
Overton. *Lanc* 1C 32
Overton. *N Yor* 1B 36
Overton. *W Yor* 1E 43
Overton. *Wrex* 4B 48
Ovingham. *Nmbd* 2F 13
Ovington. *Dur* 3A 20
Ovington. *Nmbd* 2F 13
Owler Bar. *Derbs* 1E 51
Owlerton. *S Yor* 4F 43
Owmby. *Linc* 2A 46
Owmby-by-Spital. *Linc* 4A 46
Owrytn. *Wrex* 4B 48
Owston. *S Yor* 1B 44
Owston Ferry. *N Lin* 2E 45
Owstwick. *E Yor* 3C 38
Owthorne. *E Yor* 4D 39
Owthorpe. *Notts* 4C 52
Owton Manor. *Hart* 2D 21
Oxcombe. *Linc* 1D 55
Oxenholme. *Cumb* 1A 26
Oxenhope. *W Yor* 3C 34
Oxen Park. *Cumb* 2E 25
Oxnam. *Scot* 1F 7
Oxspring. *S Yor* 2E 43
Oxton. *Mers* 4A 40
Oxton. *N Yor* 2B 36
Oxton. *Notts* 3C 52

P

Packmoor. *Stoke* 3A 50
Paddington. *Warr* 4E 41
Paddockhole. *Dum* 4A 6
Padeswood. *Flin* 2A 48
Padiham. *Lanc* 3F 33
Padside. *N Yor* 1D 35
Page Bank. *Dur* 1B 20
Painleyhill. *Staf* 4C 50
Painshawfield. *Nmbd* 2F 13
Painsthorpe. *E Yor* 1E 37
Painthorpe. *W Yor* 1F 43
Palmer Moor. *Derbs* 4D 51
Palterton. *Derbs* 2A 52
Pandy. *Wrex* 4A 48
Pannal. *N Yor* 1F 35
Pannal Ash. *N Yor* 1E 35
Pant. *Wrex* 4B 48
Pantasaph. *Flin* 1A 48
Panton. *Linc* 1B 54
Pant y Wacco. *Flin* 1A 48
Papcastle. *Cumb* 1C 16
Papplewick. *Notts* 3B 52
Parbold. *Lanc* 1C 40
Pardshaw. *Cumb* 2B 16

St Helen Auckland—Southwick

St Helen Auckland. Dur 2A 20
St Helens. Cumb 1B 16
St Helens. Mers 3C 40
St John's Chapel. Dur 1D 19
St John's Hall. Dur 1F 19
St Martin's. Shrp 4B 48
St Michael's on Wyre. Lanc 2C 32
Sale. G Man 3F 41
Saleby. Linc 1E 55
Salesbury. Lanc 3E 33
Salford. G Man 3A 42
Salkeld Dykes. Cumb 1A 18
Salmonby. Linc 1D 55
Salta. Cumb 4B 10
Saltaire. W Yor 3D 35
Saltburn-by-the-Sea. Red C 2F 21
Saltcoats. Cumb 1B 24
Salt End. E Yor 4B 38
Salter. Lanc 4B 26
Salterforth. Lanc 2A 34
Salterswall. Ches 2E 49
Saltfleet. Linc 3E 47
Saltfleetby All Saints. Linc 3E 47
Saltfleetby St Clements. Linc 3E 47
Saltfleetby St Peter. Linc 4E 47
Saltmarshe. E Yor 4D 37
Saltney. Flin 2B 48
Salton. N Yor 2A 30
Saltwick. Nmbd 1A 14
Samlesbury. Lanc 3D 33
Samlesbury Bottoms. Lanc 4E 33
Sancton. E Yor 3F 37
Sandale. Cumb 4D 11
Sandal Magna. W Yor 1F 43
Sandbach. Ches 2F 49
Sandford. Cumb 3C 18
Sandford. Shrp 4D 49
Sandhoe. Nmbd 2E 13
Sand Hole. E Yor 3E 37
Sandholme. E Yor 3E 37
Sandholme. Linc 4D 55
Sandhutton. N Yor 2C 28 (nr. Thirsk)
Sand Hutton. N Yor 1C 36 (nr. York)
Sandiacre. Derbs 4A 52
Sandilands. Linc 4F 47
Sandiway. Ches 1E 49
Sandlow Green. Ches 2F 49
Sandsend. N Yor 3B 22
Sandside. Cumb 3E 25
Sandtoft. N Lin 2D 45
Sandwick. Cumb 3F 17
Sandwith. Cumb 3A 16
Sandy Bank. Linc 3C 54
Sandycroft. Flin 2B 48
Sandyhills. Dum 3A 10
Sandylands. Lanc 4F 25
Sandystones. Scot 1D 7
Santon. Cumb 4C 16
Santon Bridge. Cumb 4C 16
Sapperton. Derbs 4D 51
Sapperton. Linc 4A 54
Satley. Dur 4A 14
Satron. N Yor 1E 27
Satterthwaite. Cumb 1E 25
Saughall. Ches 1B 48
Saughtree. Scot 3D 7
Saundby. Notts 4D 45
Sausthorpe. Linc 2D 55
Saverley Green. Staf 4B 50
Sawdon. N Yor 2C 30
Sawley. Lanc 2F 33
Sawley. N Yor 4B 28
Saxby. Linc 4A 46
Saxby All Saints. N Lin 1F 45
Saxilby. Linc 1E 53
Saxondale. Notts 4C 52
Saxton. N Yor 3A 36
Scackleton. N Yor 3F 29
Scaftworth. Notts 3C 44
Scagglethorpe. N Yor 3B 30
Scaitcliffe. Lanc 4F 33
Scalby. E Yor 4E 37
Scalby. N Yor 1D 31
Scalby Mills. N Yor 1D 31
Scaleby. Cumb 2F 11
Scaleby Hill. Cumb 2F 11
Scale Houses. Cumb 4A 12
Scales. Cumb 3D 25 (nr. Barrow-in-Furness)
Scales. Cumb 2E 17 (nr. Keswick)
Scaling. Red C 3A 22
Scaling Dam. Red C 3A 22
Scamblesby. Linc 1C 54
Scampston. N Yor 3B 30
Scampton. Linc 1F 53
Scapegoat Hill. W Yor 1C 42
Scarborough. N Yor 2D 31
Scarcliffe. Derbs 2A 52
Scarcroft. W Yor 2F 35
Scargill. Dur 3F 19
Scarisbrick. Lanc 1B 40
Scarrington. Notts 4D 53
Scarth Hill. Lanc 2C 40
Scartho. NE Lin 2C 46
Scaur. Dum 3A 10
Scawby. N Lin 2F 45
Scawby Brook. N Lin 2F 45
Scawsby. S Yor 2B 44
Scawton. N Yor 2E 29
Scholar Green. Ches 3A 50
Scholes. G Man 2E 41
Scholes. W Yor 4D 35 (nr. Bradford)
Scholes. W Yor 2D 43 (nr. Holmfirth)
Scholes. W Yor 3F 35 (nr. Leeds)
Scholey Hill. W Yor 4F 35
School Aycliffe. Darl 2B 20
School Green. Ches 2E 49
Scissett. W Yor 1E 43
Scofton. Notts 4C 44
Scopwick. Linc 3A 54
Scorborough. E Yor 2A 38
Scorton. Lanc 2D 33
Scorton. N Yor 4B 20
Scotby. Cumb 3F 11
Scotch Corner. N Yor 4B 20
Scotforth. Lanc 4F 25
Scot Hay. Staf 4A 50
Scothern. Linc 1A 54
Scot Lane End. G Man 2E 41
Scotsdike. Cumb 1E 11
Scots Gap. Nmbd 4C 8
Scotswood. Tyne 2B 14
Scotter. Linc 2E 45
Scotterthorpe. Linc 2E 45
Scotton. Linc 3E 45
Scotton. N Yor 1A 28 (nr. Catterick Garrison)
Scotton. N Yor 1F 35 (nr. Harrogate)
Scout Green. Cumb 4A 18
Scouthead. G Man 2B 42
Scrafield. Linc 2D 55
Scrainwood. Nmbd 2B 8
Scrane End. Linc 4D 55
Scrayingham. N Yor 4A 30
Scredington. Linc 4A 54
Scremby. Linc 2E 55
Scremerston. Nmbd 2C 4
Screveton. Notts 4D 53
Scrivelsby. Linc 2C 54
Scriven. N Yor 1F 35
Scronkey. Lanc 2C 32
Scrooby. Notts 3C 44
Scrub Hill. Linc 3C 54
Scruton. N Yor 1C 28
Scuggate. Cumb 1F 11
Sculcoates. Hull 3A 38
Scunthorpe. N Lin 1E 45
Seabridge. Staf 4A 50
Seaburn. Tyne 3D 15
Seacombe. Mers 3B 40
Seacroft. Linc 2F 55
Seacroft. W Yor 3F 35
Seadyke. Linc 4D 55
Seaforth. Mers 3B 40
Seaham. Dur 4D 15
Seahouses. Nmbd 3E 5
Sealand. Flin 2B 48
Seamer. N Yor 2D 31 (nr. Scarborough)
Seamer. N Yor 3D 21 (nr. Stokesley)
Searby. Linc 2A 46
Seascale. Cumb 4B 16
Seathorne. Linc 2F 55
Seathwaite. Cumb 3D 17 (nr. Borrowdale)
Seathwaite. Cumb 1D 25 (nr. Ulpha)
Seatle. Cumb 2E 25
Seatoller. Cumb 3D 17
Seaton. Cumb 1B 16
Seaton. Dur 4C 14
Seaton. E Yor 2B 38
Seaton. Nmbd 1C 14
Seaton Burn. Tyne 1B 14
Seaton Carew. Hart 2E 21
Seaton Delaval. Nmbd 1C 14
Seaton Ross. E Yor 2D 37
Seaton Sluice. Nmbd 1C 14
Seave Green. N Yor 4E 21
Seaville. Cumb 3C 10
Sebergham. Cumb 4E 11
Sedbergh. Cumb 1B 26
Sedbusk. N Yor 1D 27
Sedgebrook. Linc 4E 53
Sedgefield. Dur 2C 20
Sedgwick. Cumb 2A 26
Sefton. Mers 2B 40
Sefton Park. Mers 4B 40
Seghill. Nmbd 1B 14
Selattyn. Shrp 4A 48
Selby. N Yor 3C 36
Selside. Cumb 1A 26
Selside. N Yor 3C 26
Selston. Notts 3A 52
Serlby. Notts 4C 44
Sessay. N Yor 3D 29
Settle. N Yor 4D 27
Settrington. N Yor 3B 30
Sewerby. E Yor 4E 31
Shadforth. Dur 4C 14
Shadsworth. Bkbn 4E 33
Shadwell. W Yor 3F 35
Shafton. S Yor 1F 43
Shafton Two Gates. S Yor 1F 43
Shankhouse. Nmbd 1B 14
Shap. Cumb 3A 18
Sharlston. W Yor 1F 43
Sharlston Common. W Yor 1F 43
Sharneyford. Lanc 4A 34
Sharow. N Yor 3C 28
Sharpe Green. Lanc 3D 33
Sharperton. Nmbd 2B 8
Shatton. Derbs 4D 43
Shavington. Ches 3F 49
Shaw. G Man 2B 42
Shawdon Hall. Nmbd 1C 8
Shawforth. Lanc 4A 34
Shaw Green. Lanc 1D 41
Shawhead. Dum 1A 10
Shaw Mills. N Yor 4B 28
Shearington. Dum 2B 10
Sheen. Staf 2D 51
Sheepbridge. Derbs 1F 51
Sheep Hill. Dur 3A 14
Sheepscar. W Yor 3F 35
Sheepwash. Nmbd 4E 9
Sheffield. S Yor 4F 43
Sheffield City Airport. S Yor 4A 44
Sheldon. Derbs 2D 51
Shelf. W Yor 4D 35
Shelford. Notts 4C 52
Shelley. W Yor 1E 43
Shell Green. Hal 4D 41
Shelton. Notts 4D 53
Shepley. W Yor 2D 43
Sheraton. Dur 1D 21
Sherburn. Dur 4C 14
Sherburn. N Yor 3C 30
Sherburn Hill. Dur 4C 14
Sherburn in Elmet. N Yor 3A 36
Sheriff Hutton. N Yor 4F 29
Sherwood. Nott 4B 52
Shevington. G Man 2D 41
Shevington Moor. G Man 1D 41
Shevington Vale. G Man 2D 41
Shieldhill. Dum 1B 10
Shilbottle. Nmbd 2D 9
Shilbottle Grange. Nmbd 2E 9
Shildon. Dur 2B 20
Shillmoor. Nmbd 2A 8
Shilvington. Nmbd 4D 9
Shincliffe. Dur 4B 14
Shiney Row. Tyne 3C 14
Shipley. Derbs 4A 52
Shipley. Nmbd 1D 9
Shipley. W Yor 3D 35
Shipton. N Yor 1B 36
Shiptonthorpe. E Yor 2E 37
Shirdley Hill. Lanc 1B 40
Shire. Cumb 1B 18
Shirebrook. Derbs 2B 52
Shiregreen. S Yor 3F 43
Shiremoor. Tyne 1C 14
Shireoaks. Notts 4B 44
Shirland. Derbs 3F 51
Shirley. Derbs 4E 51
Shocklach. Ches 4C 48
Sholver. G Man 2B 42
Shopford. Cumb 1A 12
Shoresdean. Nmbd 2B 4
Shoreswood. Nmbd 2B 4
Shotley Bridge. Dur 3F 13
Shotleyfield. Nmbd 3F 13
Shottle. Derbs 4F 51
Shotton. Dur 1D 21 (nr. Peterlee)
Shotton. Dur 2C 20 (nr. Sedgefield)
Shotton. Flin 2A 48
Shotton. Nmbd 1B 14 (nr. Morpeth)
Shotton. Nmbd 3A 4 (nr. Town Yetholm)
Shotton Colliery. Dur 4C 14
Shotwick. Ches 1B 48
Shutlanehead. Staf 4A 50
Shuttlewood. Derbs 1A 52
Shuttleworth. G Man 1A 42
Sibbaldbie. Dum 4A 6
Sibsey. Linc 3D 55
Sibsey Fen Side. Linc 3D 55
Sibthorpe. Notts 4D 53
Sicklinghall. N Yor 2F 35
Siddick. Cumb 1B 16
Siddington. Ches 1A 50
Side of the Moor. G Man 1F 41
Sigglesthorne. E Yor 2B 38
Silecroft. Cumb 2C 24
Silkstone. S Yor 2E 43
Silkstone Common. S Yor 2E 43
Silksworth. Tyne 3C 14
Silk Willoughby. Linc 4A 54
Silloth. Cumb 3C 10
Sills. Nmbd 2A 8
Silpho. N Yor 1C 30
Silsden. W Yor 2C 34
Silverdale. Lanc 3F 25
Silverdale. Staf 4A 50
Silverdale Green. Lanc 3F 25
Simm's Cross. Hal 4D 41
Simm's Lane End. Mers 3D 41
Simonburn. Nmbd 1D 13
Simonstone. Lanc 3F 33
Simprim. Scot 2A 4
Sinderby. N Yor 2C 28
Sinderhope. Nmbd 3D 13
Singleton. Lanc 3B 32
Sinnington. N Yor 2A 30
Sixhills. Linc 4B 46
Skeeby. N Yor 4A 20
Skeffling. E Yor 1D 47
Skegby. Notts 2A 52 (nr. Mansfield)
Skegby. Notts 2D 53 (nr. Tuxford)
Skegness. Linc 2F 55
Skelbrooke. S Yor 1B 44
Skeldyke. Linc 4D 55
Skelfhill. Scot 2C 6
Skellingthorpe. Linc 1F 53
Skellorn Green. Ches 4B 42
Skellow. S Yor 1B 44
Skelmanthorpe. W Yor 1E 43
Skelmersdale. Lanc 2C 40
Skelton. Cumb 1F 17
Skelton. E Yor 4D 37
Skelton. N Yor 4F 19 (nr. Richmond)
Skelton. N Yor 4C 28 (nr. Ripon)
Skelton. Red C 3F 21
Skelton. York 1B 36
Skelton Green. Red C 3F 21
Skelwith Bridge. Cumb 4E 17
Skendleby. Linc 2E 55
Skendleby Psalter. Linc 1E 55
Skerne. E Yor 1A 38
Skerton. Lanc 4F 25
Skewsby. N Yor 3F 29
Skidbrooke. Linc 3E 47
Skidbrooke North End. Linc 3E 47
Skidby. E Yor 3A 38
Skinburness. Cumb 3C 10
Skinningrove. Red C 2A 22
Skippool. Lanc 2B 32
Skiprigg. Cumb 4E 11
Skipsea. E Yor 1B 38
Skipsea Brough. E Yor 1B 38
Skipton. N Yor 1B 34
Skipton-on-Swale. N Yor 3C 28
Skipwith. N Yor 3C 36
Skirbeck. Linc 4D 55
Skirbeck Quarter. Linc 4D 55
Skirlaugh. E Yor 3B 38
Skirpenbeck. E Yor 1D 37
Skirwith. Cumb 1B 18
Skirwith. N Yor 3C 26
Skitby. Cumb 2F 11
Skitham. Lanc 2C 32
Slack. W Yor 4B 34
Slackhall. Derbs 4C 42
Slack Head. Cumb 3F 25
Slackholme End. Linc 1F 55
Slack, The. Dur 2A 20
Slade Hooton. S Yor 4B 44
Slaggyford. Nmbd 3B 12
Slaidburn. Lanc 1F 33
Slaid Hill. W Yor 2F 35
Slaithwaite. W Yor 1C 42
Slaley. Derbs 3E 51
Slaley. Nmbd 3E 13
Slattock. G Man 2A 42
Sleaford. Linc 4A 54
Sleagill. Cumb 3A 18
Sledmere. E Yor 4C 30
Sleightholme. Dur 3E 19
Sleights. N Yor 4B 22
Slingsby. N Yor 3F 29
Sloothby. Linc 1E 55
Slyne. Lanc 4F 25
Smallbridge. G Man 1B 42
Smalldale. Derbs 1C 50
Smalley. Derbs 4A 52
Smallholm. Dum 1C 10
Smallwood Hey. Lanc 2B 32
Smardale. Cumb 4C 18
Smithfield. Cumb 2F 11
Smith Green. Lanc 1C 32
Smithy Bridge. G Man 1B 42
Smithy Green. Ches 1F 49
Smithy Lane Ends. Lanc 1C 40
Snainton. N Yor 2C 30
Snaith. E Yor 4C 36
Snape. N Yor 2B 28
Snape Green. Lanc 1B 40
Snarford. Linc 4A 46
Sneaton. N Yor 4B 22
Sneatonthorpe. N Yor 4C 22
Snelland. Linc 4A 46
Snelston. Derbs 4D 51
Snitter. Nmbd 2C 8
Snitterby. Linc 3F 45
Snods Edge. Nmbd 3F 13
Snydale. W Yor 1A 44
Sockbridge. Cumb 2F 17
Sockburn. Darl 4C 20
Sollom. Lanc 1C 40
Somerby. Linc 2A 46
Somercotes. Derbs 3A 52
Somersal Herbert. Derbs 4D 51
Somersby. Linc 1D 55
Sookholme. Notts 2B 52
Sotby. Linc 1C 54
Sots Hole. Linc 2B 54
Soughton. Flin 2A 48
Soulby. Cumb 3C 18 (nr. Appleby)
Soulby. Cumb 2F 17 (nr. Penrith)
Sourhope. Scot 4A 4
Soutergate. Cumb 2D 25
South Anston. S Yor 4B 44
South Bank. Red C 2E 21
South Beach. Nmbd 1C 14
South Bents. Tyne 2D 15
South Broomhill. Nmbd 3E 9
Southburn. E Yor 1F 37
South Carlton. Linc 1F 53
South Cave. E Yor 3F 37
South Charlton. Nmbd 4D 5
South Church. Dur 2B 20
South Cleatlam. Dur 3A 20
South Cliffe. E Yor 3E 37
South Clifton. Notts 1E 53
South Cockerington. Linc 4D 47
South Crosland. W Yor 1D 43
South Dalton. E Yor 2F 37
Southdean. Scot 2E 7
South Duffield. N Yor 3C 36
South Elkington. Linc 4C 46
South Elmsall. W Yor 1A 44
South End. Cumb 4D 25
South End. N Lin 4B 38
Southerfield. Cumb 4C 10
Southerness. Dum 3A 10
South Ferriby. N Lin 4F 37
South Field. E Yor 4A 38
South Hazelrigg. Nmbd 3C 4
South Hetton. Dur 4C 14
South Hiendley. W Yor 1F 43
South Holme. N Yor 3A 30
South Hykeham. Linc 2F 53
South Hylton. Tyne 3C 14
South Kelsey. Linc 3A 46
South Killingholme. N Lin 1B 46
South Kilvington. N Yor 2D 29
South Kirkby. W Yor 1A 44
South Kyme. Linc 4B 54
South Leverton. Notts 4D 45
South Middleton. Nmbd 4C 4
South Milford. N Yor 3A 36
South Moor. Dur 3A 14
South Muskham. Notts 3D 53
South Newbald. E Yor 3F 37
South Newsham. Nmbd 1C 14
South Normanton. Derbs 3A 52
South Ormsby. Linc 1D 55
South Otterington. N Yor 2C 28
South Owersby. Linc 3A 46
Southowram. W Yor 4D 35
Southport. Mers 1B 40
South Rauceby. Linc 4A 54
South Reston. Linc 4E 47
Southrey. Linc 2B 54
South Scarle. Notts 2E 53
South Shields. Tyne 2C 14
South Shore. Bkpl 3B 32
South Somercotes. Linc 3E 47
South Stainley. N Yor 4C 28
South Stainmore. Cumb 3D 19
South Thoresby. Linc 1E 55
Southwaite. Cumb 4F 11
Southwell. Notts 3C 52
South Wheatley. Notts 4D 45
Southwick. Tyne 3C 14

Westow. N Yor 4A 30
West Park. Hart 1D 21
West Pelton. Dur 3B 14
West Rainton. Dur 4C 14
West Rasen. Linc 4A 46
West Ravendale. NE Lin 3C 46
West Rounton. N Yor 4D 21
West Scrafton. N Yor 2F 27
West Sleekburn. Nmbd 4E 9
West Stockwith. Notts 3D 45
West Stonesdale. N Yor 4D 19
West Tanfield. N Yor 3B 28
West Thirston. Nmbd 2D 9
West Torrington. Linc 4B 46
West View. Hart 1E 21
Westville. Notts 4B 52
Westward. Cumb 4D 11
Westwick. Dur 3F 19
West Willoughby. Linc 4F 53
West Witton. N Yor 2F 27
West Woodburn. Nmbd 4A 8
West Woodside. Cumb 4E 11
Westwoodside. N Lin 3D 45
West Wylam. Nmbd 2A 14
Wetheral. Cumb 3F 11
Wetherby. W Yor 2A 36
Wetley Rocks. Staf 4B 50
Wettenhall. Ches 2E 49
Wetton. Staf 3D 51
Wetwang. E Yor 1F 37
Wetwood. Staf 4F 49
Whale. Cumb 2A 18
Whaley. Derbs 1B 52
Whaley Bridge. Derbs 4C 42
Whaley Thorns. Derbs 1B 52
Whalley. Lanc 3F 33
Whalton. Nmbd 4D 9
Wham. N Yor 4C 26
Wharfe. N Yor 4C 26
Wharles. Lanc 3C 32
Wharncliffe Side. S Yor 3E 43
Wharram-le-Street. N Yor 4B 30
Wharton. Ches 2E 49
Washashton. N Yor 4A 20
Whasset. Cumb 2A 26
Whatstandwell. Derbs 3F 51
Whatton. Notts 4D 53
Whaw. N Yor 4E 19
Wheatcroft. Derbs 3F 51
Wheatley. W Yor 4C 34
Wheatley Hill. Dur 1C 20
Wheatley Lane. Lanc 3A 34
Wheatley Park. S Yor 2B 44
Wheelock. Ches 3F 49
Wheelock Heath. Ches 3F 49
Wheelton. Lanc 4E 33
Wheldrake. York 2C 36
Whelpo. Cumb 1E 17
Whelston. Flin 1A 48
Whenby. N Yor 4F 29
Wheston. Derbs 1D 51
Whicham. Cumb 2C 24
Whickham. Tyne 2B 14
Whin Lane End. Lanc 2B 32
Whinny Hill. Stoc T 3C 20
Whirlow. S Yor 4F 43
Whisby. Linc 2F 53
Whisterfield. Ches 1A 50
Whiston. Mers 3C 40
Whiston. S Yor 3A 44
Whiston. Staf 4C 50
Whiston Eaves. Staf 4C 50
Whitbeck. Cumb 2C 24
Whitburn. Tyne 2D 15
Whitburn Colliery. Tyne 2D 15
Whitby. Ches 1B 48
Whitby. N Yor 3B 22
Whitbyheath. Ches 1B 48
Whitchurch. Shrp 4D 49

White Chapel. Lanc 2D 33
White Coppice. Lanc 1E 41
Whitefield. G Man 2A 42
Whitegate. Ches 2E 49
Whitehaven. Cumb 3A 16
Whitehough. Derbs 4C 42
White Kirkley. Dur 1F 19
White Lee. W Yor 4E 35
White Pit. Linc 1D 55
Whiteside. Nmbd 2C 12
Whitewall Corner. N Yor 3A 30
Whitewell. Lanc 2E 33
Whitewell Bottom. Lanc 4A 34
Whitfield. Nmbd 3C 12
Whitgift. E Yor 4E 37
Whitford. Flin 1A 48
Whitgift. E Yor 4E 37
Whitkirk. W Yor 3F 35
Whitley. N Yor 4B 36
Whitley Bay. Tyne 1C 14
Whitley Chapel. Nmbd 3E 13
Whitley Lower. W Yor 1E 43
Whitley Thorpe. N Yor 4B 36
Whitmore. Staf 4A 50
Whitrigg. Cumb 3D 11
(nr. Kirkbride)
Whitrigg. Cumb 1D 17
(nr. Torpenhow)
Whitsome. Scot 1A 4
Whittingham. Nmbd 1C 8
Whittington. Derbs 1A 52
Whittington. Lanc 3B 26
Whittle-le-Woods. Lanc 4D 33
Whittlestone Head. Bkbn 1F 41
Whitton. N Lin 4F 37
Whitton. Nmbd 2C 8
Whitton. Scot 4A 4
Whitton. Stoc T 2C 20
Whittonstall. Nmbd 3F 13
Whitwell. Derbs 1B 52
Whitwell. N Yor 1B 28
Whitwell-on-the-Hill.
N Yor 4A 30
Whitwood. W Yor 4A 36
Whitworth. Lanc 1A 42
Whixall. Shrp 4D 49
Whixley. N Yor 1A 36
Whorlton. Dur 3A 20
Whorlton. N Yor 4D 21
Whygate. Nmbd 1C 12
Wickenby. Linc 4A 46
Wickersley. S Yor 3A 44
Widdrington. Nmbd 3E 9
Widdrington Station.
Nmbd 3E 9
Wide Open. Tyne 1B 14
Widnes. Hal 4D 41
Wigan. G Man 2D 41
Wigginton. York 1B 36
Wigglesworth. N Yor 1A 34
Wiggonby. Cumb 3D 11
Wighill. N Yor 2A 36
Wigsley. Notts 1E 53
Wigtoft. Linc 4C 54
Wigton. Cumb 4D 11
Wigtwizzle. S Yor 3E 43
Wike. W Yor 2F 35
Wilberfoss. E Yor 1D 37
Wildboarclough. Ches 2B 50
Wilderspool. Warr 4E 41
Wildsworth. Linc 3E 45
Wilford. Nott 4B 52
Wilkesley. Ches 4E 49
Wilksby. Linc 2C 54
Willaston. Ches 3E 49
(nr. Crewe)
Willaston. Ches 1B 48
(nr. Neston)
Willerby. E Yor 3A 38
Willerby. N Yor 3D 31

Willingham by Stow. Linc 4E 45
Willington. Dur 1A 20
Willington. Tyne 2C 14
Willington Corner. Ches 2D 49
Willitoft. E Yor 3D 37
Willoughbridge. Staf 4F 49
Willoughby. Linc 1E 55
Willoughton. Linc 3F 45
Wilmslow. Ches 4A 42
Wilpshire. Lanc 3E 33
Wilsden. W Yor 3C 34
Wilsford. Linc 4A 54
Wilsill. N Yor 4A 28
Wilsthorpe. E Yor 4E 31
Wilton. Cumb 3B 16
Wilton. N Yor 2B 30
Wilton. Red C 3E 21
Wilton. Scot 1D 7
Wincle. Ches 2D 55
Wincham. Ches 1E 49
Wincle. Ches 2B 50
Windermere. Cumb 1F 25
Windle Hill. Ches 1B 48
Windley. Derbs 4F 51
Windmill. Derbs 1D 51
Windyharbour. Ches 1A 50
Winestead. E Yor 4D 39
Wingate. Dur 1C 20
Wingates. G Man 2E 41
Wingates. Nmbd 3D 9
Wingerworth. Derbs 2F 51
Wingfield Park. Derbs 3F 51
Winkburn. Notts 3D 53
Winkhill. Staf 3C 50
Winksley. N Yor 3B 28
Winlaton. Tyne 2A 14
Winlaton Mill. Tyne 2A 14
Winmarleigh. Lanc 2C 32
Winnington. Ches 1E 49
Winnington. Staf 4F 49
Winnothdale. Staf 4C 50
Winscales. Cumb 2B 16
Winsford. Ches 2E 49
Winskill. Cumb 1A 18
Winster. Cumb 1F 25
Winster. Derbs 2E 51
Winston. Dur 3A 20
Winterburn. N Yor 1B 34
Winteringham. N Lin 4F 37
Winterley. Ches 3F 49
Wintersett. W Yor 1F 43
Winterton. N Lin 1F 45
Winthorpe. Linc 2F 55
Winthorpe. Notts 3E 53
Winton. Cumb 3C 18
Wintringham. N Yor 3B 30
Winwick. Warr 3E 41
Wirksworth. Derbs 3E 51
Wirswall. Ches 4D 49
Wiseton. Notts 4D 45
Wispington. Linc 1C 54
Wistaston. Ches 3E 49
Wistow. N Yor 3B 36
Wiswell. Lanc 3F 33
Witham St Hughs. Linc 2E 53
Withcall. Linc 4C 46
Withern. Linc 4E 47
Withernsea. E Yor 4D 39
Withernwick. E Yor 2B 38
Witherslack. Cumb 2F 25
Withington. G Man 3A 42
Withington. Staf 4C 50
Withington Green. Ches 1A 50
Withnell. Lanc 4E 33
Withnell Fold. Lanc 4E 33
Witton Gilbert. Dur 4B 14
Witton-le-Wear. Dur 1A 20
Witton Park. Dur 1A 20
Wold Newton. E Yor 3D 31

Wold Newton. NE Lin 3C 46
Wollaton. Nott 4B 52
Wolsingham. Dur 1F 19
Wolstanton. Staf 4A 50
Wolsty. Cumb 3C 10
Wolviston. Stoc T 2D 21
Wombleton. N Yor 2F 29
Wombwell. S Yor 2F 43
Womersley. N Yor 1B 44
Woodale. N Yor 3F 27
Woodall. S Yor 4A 44
Woodbank. Ches 1B 48
Woodbeck. Notts 1D 53
Woodborough. Notts 4C 52
Woodchurch. Mers 4A 40
Woodend. Cumb 1C 24
Wood Enderby. Linc 2C 54
Woodfields. Lanc 3E 33
Woodford. G Man 4A 42
Wood Hall. E Yor 3B 38
Woodhall. Linc 2C 54
Woodhall. N Yor 1E 27
Woodhall Spa. Linc 2B 54
Woodhorn. Nmbd 4F 9
Woodhouse. S Yor 4A 44
Woodhouse. W Yor 3E 35
(nr. Leeds)
Woodhouse. W Yor 4F 35
(nr. Normanton)
Woodhouses. Ches 1D 49
Woodhouses. G Man 2B 42
(nr. Failsworth)
Woodhouses. G Man 3F 41
(nr. Sale)
Woodland. Dur 2F 19
Woodlands. N Yor 1F 35
Woodlands. S Yor 2B 44
Woodlesford. W Yor 4F 35
Woodley. G Man 3B 42
Woodmansey. E Yor 3A 38
Woodplumpton. Lanc 3D 33
Woodrow. Cumb 4D 11
Wood Row. W Yor 4F 35
Woodsetts. S Yor 4B 44
Woodside. Cumb 1B 16
Woodside. Derbs 4F 51
Woodside. Dum 1B 10
Woodside. Dur 2A 20
Woodthorpe. Derbs 1A 52
Woodthorpe. Linc 4E 47
Woodthorpe. York 2B 36
Woodvale. Mers 1B 40
Woodale. W Yor 2D 43
Wooler. Nmbd 4B 4
Woolley. Derbs 2F 51
Woolley. W Yor 1F 43
Woolsington. Tyne 2A 14
Woolsthorpe. Linc 4E 53
Woolston. Warr 3E 41
Woolton. Mers 4C 40
Wooperton. Nmbd 4C 4
Woore. Shrp 4F 49
Wootton. N Lin 1A 46
Wootton. Staf 4D 51
Woottons. Staf 4C 50
Workington. Cumb 2A 16
Worksop. Notts 1B 52
Worlaby. N Lin 1A 46
Worleston. Ches 3E 49
Wormhill. Derbs 1D 51
Worrall. S Yor 3F 43
Worsbrough. S Yor 2F 43
Worsley. G Man 2F 41
Worsthorne. Lanc 3A 34
Worston. Lanc 2F 33
Worthenbury. Wrex 4C 48
Wortley. S Yor 3F 43
Wortley. W Yor 3E 35
Worton. N Yor 1E 27

Wragby. Linc 1B 54
Wragby. W Yor 1A 44
Wrangbrook. W Yor 1A 44
Wrangle. Linc 3E 55
Wrangle Lowgate. Linc 3E 55
Wrawby. N Lin 2A 46
Wray. Lanc 4B 26
Wrayton. Lanc 3B 26
Wrea Green. Lanc 3B 32
Wreay. Cumb 4F 11
(nr. Carlisle)
Wreay. Cumb 2F 17
(nr. Penrith)
Wrecsam. Wrex 3B 48
Wrekenton. Tyne 3B 14
Wrelton. N Yor 2A 30
Wrenbury. Ches 4D 49
Wrenthorpe. W Yor 4F 35
Wressle. E Yor 3D 37
Wressle. N Lin 2F 45
Wrexham. Wrex 3B 48
Wrexham Industrial Estate.
Wrex 4B 48
Wrightlington Bar. Lanc 1D 41
Wrinehill. Staf 4F 49
Wroot. N Lin 2D 45
Wyaston. Derbs 4D 51
Wybers Wood. NE Lin 2C 46
Wyberton. Linc 4D 55
Wybunbury. Ches 4E 49
Wycliffe. Dur 3A 20
Wyke. W Yor 4D 35
Wykeham. N Yor 3B 30
(nr. Malton)
Wykeham. N Yor 2C 30
(nr. Scarborough)
Wylam. Nmbd 2A 14
Wythenshawe. G Man 4A 42
Wythop Mill. Cumb 2C 16
Wyton. E Yor 3B 38

Y

Yaddlethorpe. N Lin 2E 45
Yafforth. N Yor 1C 28
Yanwath. Cumb 2A 18
Yapham. E Yor 1D 37
Yarburgh. Linc 3D 47
Yarm. Stoc T 3D 21
Yarnow. Nmbd 4F 7
Yarrow. Nmbd 4F 7
Yarrow Feus. Scot 1B 6
Yeadon. W Yor 2E 35
Yealand Conyers. Lanc 3A 26
Yealand Redmayne. Lanc 3A 26
Yearby. Red C 2F 21
Yearngill. Cumb 4C 10
Yearsley. N Yor 3E 29
Yeaveley. Derbs 4D 51
Yeavering. Nmbd 3B 4
Yedingham. N Yor 3B 30
Yeldersley Hollies. Derbs 4E 51
Yetlington. Nmbd 2C 8
Y Fflint. Flin 1A 48
Yockenthwaite. N Yor 3E 27
Yokefleet. E Yor 4E 37
York. York 1C 36
Youlgreave. Derbs 2E 51
Youlthorpe. E Yor 1D 37
Youlton. N Yor 4D 29
Young Wood. Linc 1B 54
Yr Hob. Flin 3B 48
Yr Wyddgrug. Flin 2A 48
Ysceifiog. Flin 1A 48
Y Waun. Wrex 4A 48

SAFETY CAMERA INFORMATION

Safety camera locations are publicised by the Safer Roads Partnership who operate them in order to encourage drivers to comply with speed limits at these sites. It is the driver's absolute responsibility to be aware of and to adhere to speed limits at all times.

By showing this safety camera information it is the intention of Geographers' A-Z Map Company Ltd., to encourage safe driving and greater awareness of speed limits and vehicle speed. Data accurate at time of printing.

CITY & TOWN CENTRE PLANS

Reference to Town Plans

MOTORWAY	M6	BUS STATION	
MOTORWAY UNDER CONSTRUCTION		CAR PARK (Selection of)	P
MOTORWAY JUNCTIONS WITH NUMBERS		CHURCH	†
Unlimited Interchange	4	CITY WALL	
Limited Interchange	5	FERRY (Vehicular)	
PRIMARY ROUTE	A55	(Foot only)	
PRIMARY ROUTE JUNCTION WITH NUMBER	32	GOLF COURSE	
DUAL CARRIAGEWAYS		HELIPORT	
CLASS A ROAD	A675	HOSPITAL	H
CLASS B ROAD	B5248	INFORMATION CENTRE	i
MAJOR ROADS UNDER CONSTRUCTION		LIGHTHOUSE	
MAJOR ROADS PROPOSED		MARKET	
MINOR ROADS		NATIONAL TRUST PROPERTY (Open)	NT
RESTRICTED ACCESS		(Restricted opening)	NT
PEDESTRIANIZED ROAD & MAIN FOOTWAY		(National Trust of Scotland)	NTS NTS
ONE WAY STREETS		PARK & RIDE	P+
TOLL	TOLL	PLACE OF INTEREST	
RAILWAY AND B.R. STATION		POLICE STATION	▲
UNDERGROUND / METRO & D.L.R. STATION	DLR	POST OFFICE	★
LEVEL CROSSING AND TUNNEL		SHOPPING AREA (Main street and precinct)	
TRAM STOP AND ONE WAY TRAM STOP		SHOPMOBILITY	
BUILT-UP AREA		TOILET	▼
ABBEY, CATHEDRAL, PRIORY ETC.	†	VIEWPOINT	

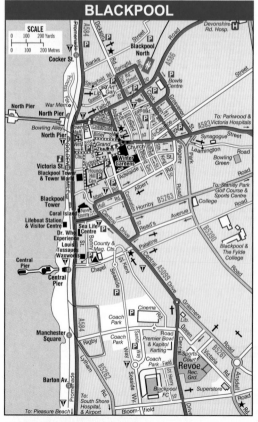

BLACKPOOL

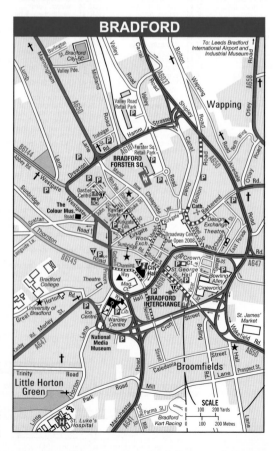

BRADFORD

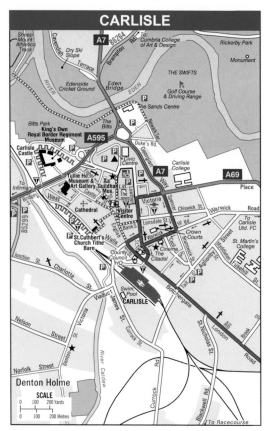

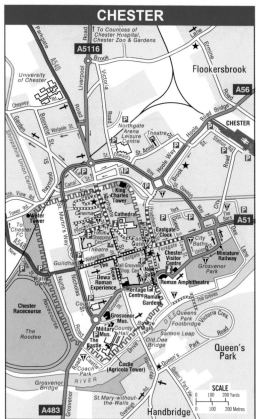

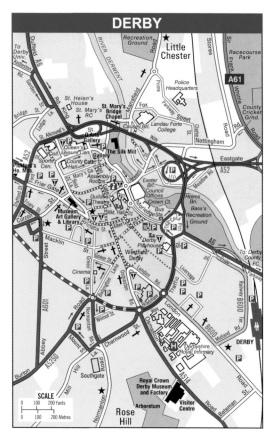

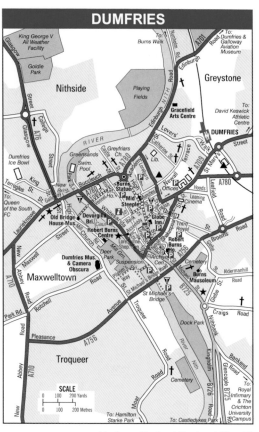

DURHAM

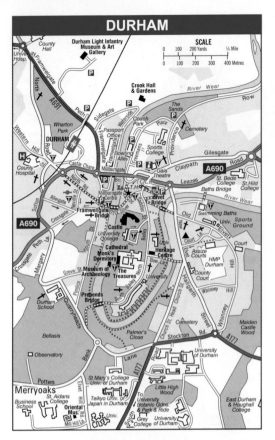

HARROGATE

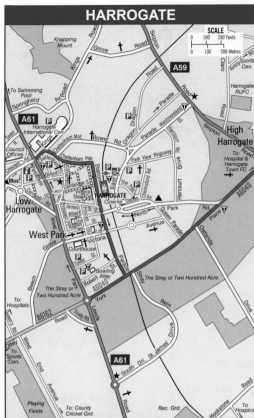

KINGSTON UPON HULL

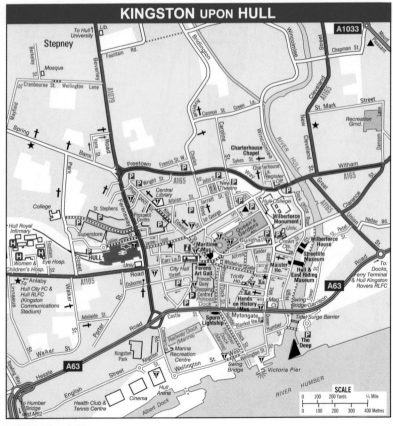

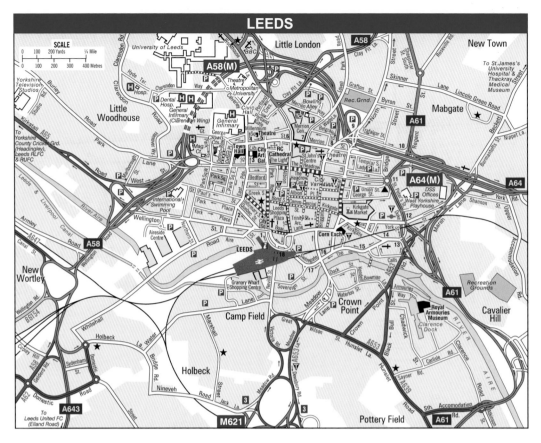

LEEDS

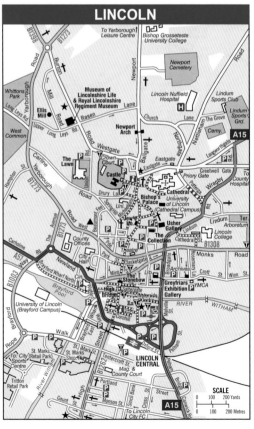

LINCOLN

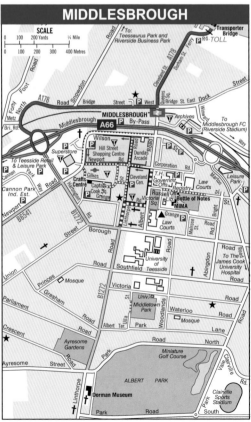

MIDDLESBROUGH

Northern England Regional Atlas 75

LIVERPOOL

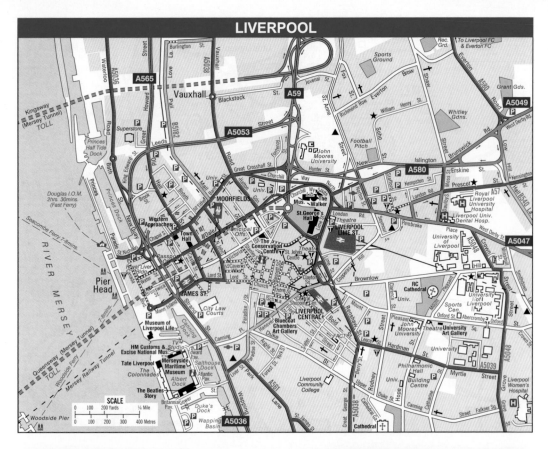

MANCHESTER

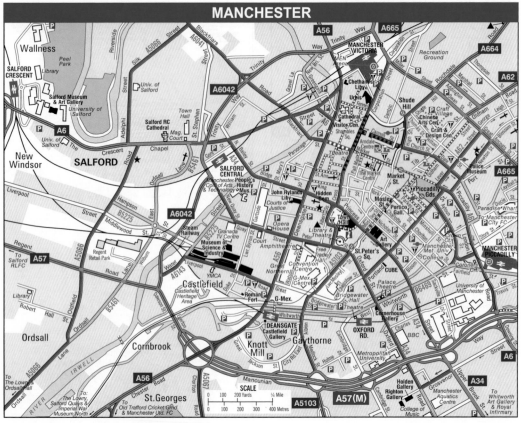

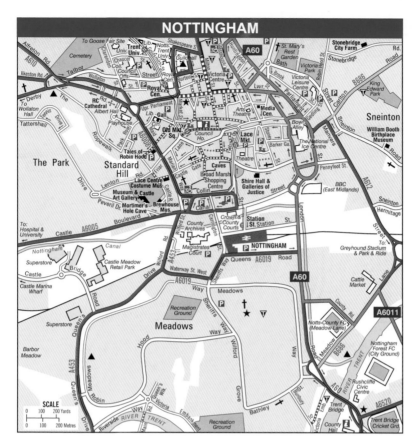

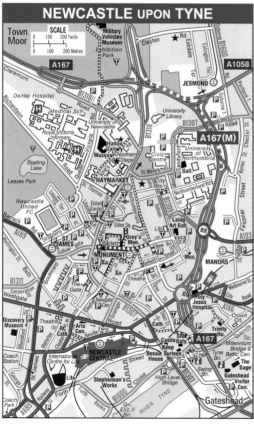

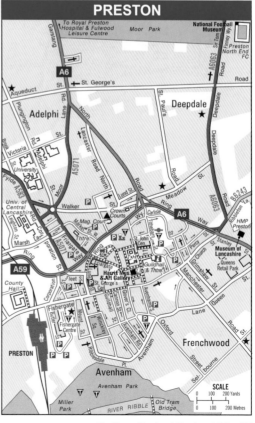

SHEFFIELD

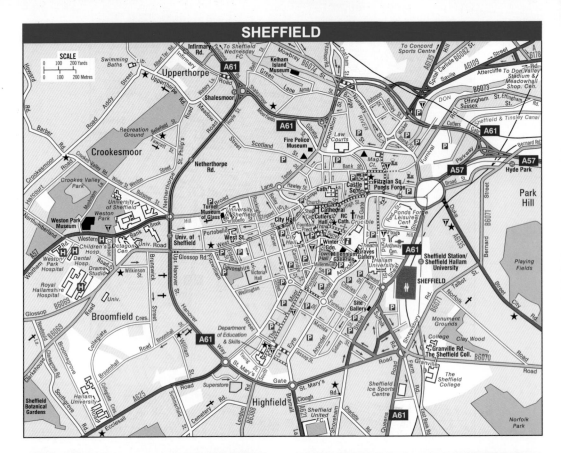

STOKE-ON-TRENT

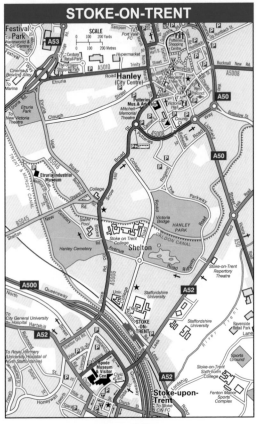

SUNDERLAND

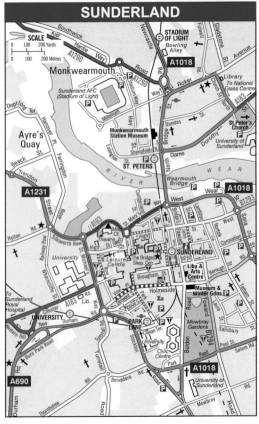

YORK

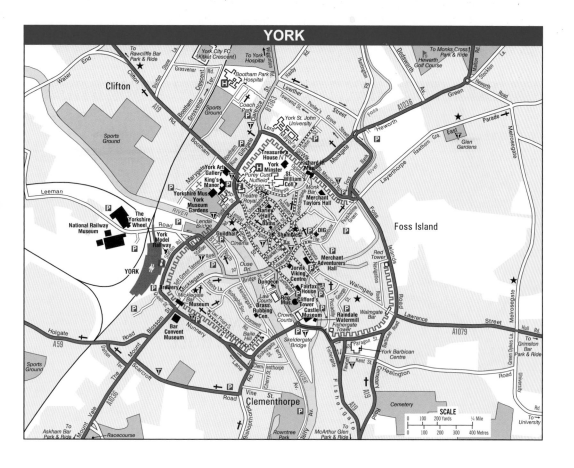

MANCHESTER AIRPORT

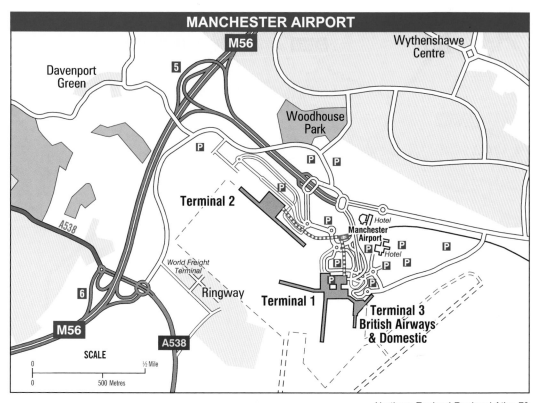

KINGSTON UPON HULL

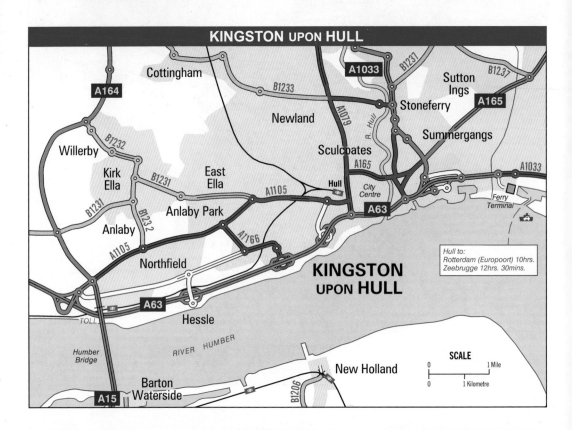

Cottingham

A164

B1233

A1033

B1231

Sutton Ings

B1237

A165

Stoneferry

Summergangs

Willerby

B1232

Newland

A1019

Sculcoates

R. Hull

A1033

Kirk Ella

B1231

East Ella

A1105

A165

City Centre

Ferry Terminal

B1231

B1232

Anlaby Park

Hull

Anlaby

A1166

A63

KINGSTON UPON HULL

A1105

Northfield

Hull to:
Rotterdam (Europoort) 10hrs.
Zeebrugge 12hrs. 30mins.

TOLL

A63

Hessle

Humber Bridge

RIVER HUMBER

New Holland

SCALE

0 ___ 1 Mile

0 ___ 1 Kilometre

Barton Waterside

A15

B1206

NEWCASTLE UPON TYNE

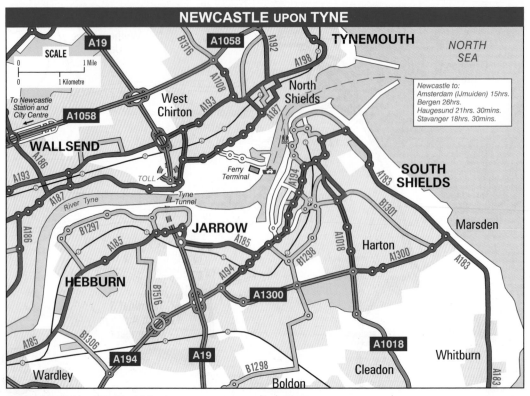

A19

B1316

A1058

A192

TYNEMOUTH

NORTH SEA

SCALE

0 ___ 1 Mile

0 ___ 1 Kilometre

A198

A1108

North Shields

Newcastle to:
Amsterdam (IJmuiden) 15hrs.
Bergen 26hrs.
Haugesund 21hrs. 30mins.
Stavanger 18hrs. 30mins.

West Chirton

A193

To Newcastle Station and City Centre

A1058

A187

WALLSEND

A186

Ferry Terminal

A194

SOUTH SHIELDS

A193

TOLL

A183

A187

River Tyne

Tyne Tunnel

A185

JARROW

A185

B1301

Marsden

A186

B1297

A194

B1298

A1018

Harton

A1300

A183

HEBBURN

B1516

A194

A1300

A185

B1306

A194

A19

B1298

A1018

Cleadon

Whitburn

A183

Wardley

Boldon